3.95

# CHILDREN, GRIEF AN

01

# THE PRACTICE OF SOCIAL WORK SERIES

*General editors: Bill Jordan and Jean Packman*

1  MATE AND STALEMATE
Janet Mattinson and Ian Sinclair

2  GROWING UP IN CARE: TEN PEOPLE TALKING
Barbara Kahan

3  CREATIVE SOCIAL WORK
David Brandon and Bill Jordan, editors

4  CHILDREN, GRIEF AND SOCIAL WORK
Gill Lonsdale, Peter Elfer and Rod Ballard

# Children, Grief and Social Work

GILL LONSDALE, PETER ELFER
AND ROD BALLARD

Basil Blackwell · Oxford

First published 1979 by
Basil Blackwell Publisher
5 Alfred Street
Oxford OX1 4HB
England

ISBN  0 631 12191 9
0 631 12181 1 Paperback

Printed in Great Britain by
Billing and Sons Limited.
London, Guildford and Worcester.

# Contents

Introduction
*Bill Jordan*                                                     vii

1  Helping Parents at the Birth and
   Death of their Handicapped Child                                 1
   *Gill Lonsdale*

2  Social Work with Children with
   Leukaemia and their Families                                    75
   *Peter Elfer*

3  Face to Face with the Unthinkable                              115
   *Rod Ballard*

Glossary of Medical Terms                                         125

Index                                                             127

# Introduction

Each of the three essays in this book contains all the elements in the title – children, grief and social work. Gill Lonsdale's piece is about a project to help parents in the period immediately following the birth (and in some cases death) of a handicapped child. Peter Elfer's is concerned with the lives of families with children diagnosed as having leukaemia. Rod Ballard, himself a social worker, writes about the experience of having a mentally handicapped child.

The grief experienced by all these people was caused by irreparable loss – the loss of a healthy child. Nothing a social worker could do would make good this loss, or reduce the pain associated with it. Yet paradoxically there is little dispute among social workers about the value of offering help in such situations, and the opinions of most clients who received social work help in these samples supported the professional viewpoint. What these essays analyse, therefore, is how help can best be given.

All three of the essays are very upsetting to read. The death of a child was standard material for providing pathos in Victorian novels. These deaths, and the sufferings of the parents of handicapped children, are no less moving, and more shocking, because such things are uncommon today. But it is not only grief that moves us; we are affected also by the courage of the parents, children and social workers. This alone seems to make some sense of the otherwise meaningless and wanton cruelty of disease and deformity.

Gill Lonsdale teaches social work, as does Rod Ballard; Peter Elfer was a student on a social work course when he did his study. They describe different groups of children, with different needs. But the common theme running through their separate accounts is the need for social workers to be available, with compassion and comfort, to families suddenly confronted with these kinds of catastrophes. This is not a newly-discovered need; in the closer-knit communities of the past it was met by kin and neighbours.

All three authors emphasise that humility and respect are more valued qualities in such work than flashy therapeutic skills. Social workers do not "know the right way" for people to react in such circumstances, still less should they impose their stereotyped formulae on others' suffering. Rather they are there to help people find their own way through their crises, and to provide a substitute for or complement to the fellow-feeling once given mainly by the afflicted to each other.

In his novel 'Bleak House', Dickens describes the scene in an impoverished brickmaker's hovel, immediately after the death of a baby. 'An ugly woman, very poorly clothed, hurried in while I was glancing at them, and coming straight up to the mother, said, 'Jenny! Jenny!' The mother rose on being so addressed, and fell upon the woman's neck. She also had upon her face and arms the marks of ill-usage. She had no kind of grace about her, but the grace of sympathy; but when she condoled with the woman, and her own tears fell, she wanted no beauty. I say condoled, but her only words were, 'Jenny! Jenny!' All the rest was in the tone in which she said them.'

Of course most families in present-day society can still draw the equivalent of this comfort from neighbours and kin, as these essays illustrate. But even some who had such a network of support needed something more — an outsider who would listen longer or better, who would let them discover the heart of their feelings, and who had links with the mysterious and intimidating world of medicine. And however much this work has become professionalized since Dickens' time, the authors show that the spirit of his comforter is as relevant as ever.

.BILL JORDAN

# Helping Parents
## at the Birth and Death
## of their Handicapped Child

GILL LONSDALE

*All happy families are alike but an unhappy family is unhappy after its own fashion.* TOLSTOY: ANNA KARENIN

A handicapped child could be born into any family. It can happen in the aristocracy and in the working class, to intellectual parents and to the less able, to white people or to coloured, and although the risk increases as a mother gets older, young couples also give birth to children who are impaired. It is a random risk for the whole population that approximately 3 in every 100 children born will be handicapped; and this means that the family of every one of these children is likely to be a handicapped family. No matter how easy the handicapped child is to manage or how much he is loved and accepted by the family, his arrival will completely alter their whole way of life and create continuing and far-reaching problems.

In backgrounds of such diversity it would seem unlikely that the arrival of a handicapped child would create similar problems in all the families. It is known that some parents cope and some do not, but as yet we have little explanation of the reasons for this. It might be that there are links between being able to manage and having adequate finances, or with enjoying secure relationships within the family, or with the nature of the handicap itself, or it might be a combination of all three. The nature of the problems suggest that it is an area for social work involvement but of what kind and when it is likely to be most helpful has perhaps been insufficiently considered.

1

In an attempt to understand more about the needs of families with handicapped children I used a detailed questionnaire and a tape recorder to interview a sample of sixty families each with a handicapped child under the age of twelve. All lived within one city, and the children were or had been patients at the same city's hospital. Most of the families had lived in the city since the child had been born and those who had moved into the area subsequently generally were agreed that the services they had experienced there were better than they had known elsewhere. These families as consumers of the services and chief judges of the outcome can provide information particularly relevant to future planning. This applies especially to social work; we still know very little about its meaning, and if we are to be more sure of the meaning then the client's viewpoint must be very important.

One of the most significant findings of the survey was that so many of the parents thought *the way they had been treated* when they were told of their child's condition was far worse than the content of the information. As perhaps is to be expected, the parents remembered very clearly who it was who had told them about their child. Possibly with the passage of time and the displaced anger of the crisis parents remembered less clearly what was said, and this is not very important. What is important is that their recollections tended to be predominantly negative and seemingly some situations were handled rather insensitively if the parents were left with the feeling that it had been an awful experience. Obviously the actual conveying of the information about having a handicapped child and the help given at this stage will have long term consequences for the overall acceptance of the situation and as such could be the most crucial time for social work help.

Some conditions are obvious at birth or very soon afterwards; in others the handicap only gradually becomes apparent as a child is slow in reaching his milestones. For the latter group of parents the telling was more traumatic with scars of it still often very apparent. These parents had bonded to a normal child believing this to be what they had. Then they learned that their child was handicapped, and for them the acceptance was harder and tended to be accompanied with much bitterness and anger. The main complaint from parents was the delay in being told that something was wrong, especially when many of them had had early suspicions that all was not well. Often when they were in hospital the suspicions were raised not by the child's appearance, nor by his behaviour, but by slight variations in hospital routine. Several mothers spoke of being put into rooms on their own and not understanding why this should be done. Others recalled having their baby 'taken away'; when they enquired about it they were told that everything was all right and that they were not to worry, which caused just the opposite reaction. Occasionally there was criticism of the bluntness with which the information was given to them. Many couples were angry when the mothers were informed on their own, more so when it had been known that the father would be coming to visit later in the day. Some parents felt that they had had difficulty in obtaining the true facts of the situation and admitted to having to resort to more clandestine ways of finding about about their child. One family had steamed open a letter from the Educational Psychologist and found out that their son was severely mentally handicapped; another had read the suspected diagnosis on the form for the Pathology Laboratory and they had been so terrified by what they saw that they went straight to the public library and read up the details in a medical dictionary.

It is already well documented that the telling of parents must be done with great sensitivity and skill (D'Arcy, McAndrew, Kew) and this is further reinforced by the comments I collected from this group of parents. There were many links to be made between the way they had been handled at this stage and the attitudes they subsequently were to adopt towards their children and their handicaps. The message which came out very clearly was that the telling should be done with honesty as early as possible, with both parents together and with plenty of time available for talking about it.

A leader in a recent British Medical Journal states:

> Telling the mother and the father is a horrid task, and however sympathetically done there is a feeling of incompetence. The essential motivation of medicine is to relieve suffering and here is a denial of that possibility. The response of all is usually to withdraw and not communicate, the well known phenomena of rejection. Often the persons most affected emotionally are unwittingly ignored.

Implicit in this quotation is the need for additional expertise; no one person can have all the skills and knowledge necessary. The survey findings indicated very clearly that the actual telling of parents needed to be improved upon and it could be that by developing social work skills in this area to complement the medical involvement some of the apparent need may be met. There was much to suggest that a multidisciplinary approach might be required.

For one year I was attached to the Social Work Department at the city hospital, taking referrals of any newly born or newly diagnosed handicapped child. Although it was known to the hospital staff that I was collecting research data, to the parents I was the social worker who specialized in the problems of handicapped children. In line with the falling birth rate, the numbers of handicapped children being born is dropping and there were fewer children confirmed as being handicapped in the year of my study compared with previous years. The work flow was not such that it would warrant a full time specialist worker in normal circumstances, but it enabled me to be readily available. When I was not in hospital I encouraged my medical colleagues to contact me at home any time during the night or weekends, and apart from taking three weeks holiday during the twelve months, I was 'on call' at all times.

During the year I was attempting to use the feedback from the survey together with conceptualizations concerning crisis, loss and bereavement as a basis for understanding and intervening at the time of telling new parents that their child was handicapped. It was an attempt to give a better service by working as a multidisciplinary team and then in due course to review whether or not this was more helpful to parents in their overall acceptance of the situation. It necessitated social work practice approximating to the medical model of total coverage rather than the more usual office hour availability, and this obviously would have implications for social work departments that would mean moving towards rota coverage.

When parents are told that their child is handicapped they face an emotional crisis as acute as any clinical challenge the handicap may present, and as much skill must be applied to the care of the parents as to the child's medical problems. The child who is handicapped is very much the patient of the doctors and nurses; the parents need the care of the social worker. Treating the family as a whole is beyond the expertise of either discipline; so there must be a team effort in which the medical knowledge is complemented by the social work skills. The team was deliberately kept small and usually consisted of one of the paediatric consultants, the social worker joined by either the registrar or the houseman. Sometimes if ongoing hospitalization was going to be necessary a Sister was also involved.

In telling parents that their child is handicapped the crisis situation is predictable and its onset controllable. Even if they have had some anxieties, parents are not strictly 'in crisis' until they are given this information. However, its content is of such enormous significance that they are likely to be thrown into immediate crisis once they are told. So with this degree of controllability it was important for the team to be operating at its most effective. Ideally telling the parents was carefully planned so that the event was as soon after the diagnosis was known to the clinicians as was reasonable, but at a time when both parents were together and those concerned were unrushed so that the parents were given all the time they needed in the immediate situation.

Parents in a shocked state retain very little of what is said initially to them. One reason why it was important for the social worker to hear exactly what information was given was so that in the days ahead this could be repeated as the parents became able to absorb a little more. But the presence of the social worker at this key interview had much greater significance. It enabled social work with the parents to be begun at the time of their maximum disequilibrium, when they seemed most in need of help and more amenable to influence. It is a case of striking while the iron is hot. It was to be shown that a short period of work timed appropriately was infinitely more effective than those situations in which parents were not seen by the team at the crisis point and were subsequently in need of much more time.

Handicap and mourning are intextricably linked. The birth of an obviously severely impaired child is often accompanied by a sound of silence followed by *sotto voce* discussion among midwives and doctors and a quick removal and separation of baby from the mother. The mother, and the father if he has been present at the delivery, know that something is wrong. Just how wrong they may have to wait to know, but from that moment a psychological process is set in motion. Parents begin a grief reaction to the loss of something they had been anticipating for nine months or longer, and that is a normal baby. Part of the aim when telling parents is to facilitate the grieving process that follows, and the main role of the social worker is to help the parents grieve in a healthy way. Although the fear of abnormality may fleetingly pass through the mind of a pregnant woman the image of the baby which she carries is generally of a normal one. When she and her husband learn that this normal baby has not been delivered to them they experience a tremendous feeling of loss. They have a baby, but it is not the baby they had visualized and they mourn the loss of normal growth and development through childhood to adult life. Their hopes and their forward planning are shattered; they face a future dominated by fear of the unknown.

A very real factor in the birth of a severely handicapped child is that he may die during the neonatal or immediate post neonatal period. These parents have to face two losses, one being the normal baby they had expected, to be followed by the death of the abnormal baby who was delivered to them. For most of these parents death of a close relative is a new experience. They are young, their own parents are usually alive and they have not encountered loss through death in their life experience, so have little to draw upon. Already they are in a grieving stage as they mourn the loss of the normal baby, and suddenly on top of this comes a second loss that is more definite and final. As they mourn the first loss there is always a part of them which will hang on to the comforting thought that perhaps the doctors are wrong and it is not as bad as they say. It could be that their baby will make better progress than they had been lead to believe. But when that baby dies there is nothing left to hope for and they are totally bereaved. Yet at the same time they experience ambivalent feelings, for while a part of them knows that death perhaps was the best way out, a part of them believes that they could have done much for that child.

Inevitably bereavement is one of the severest forms of psychological stress. It is the price that is paid for commitment, and the pain of grief is as much a part of life as the joy of love. A couple may have committed themselves to parenthood only to find that so very soon they have lost that status. The death of a child is untimely, and the psychological adjustment of the family is likely to be less good than in timely death. There is also very little to remember, and memories are an essential part of the mourning process, something to which people in their grief can return. Death represents the ultimate loss and arouses powerful states not only in the immediate relatives but in the staff involved with the caring. I found that sometimes the doctors and nurses look to the social worker for support as well. Perhaps one of the benefits of having a small case load with a high proportion of grief and mourning was that it gave me a chance to recharge my own emotional batteries. As a team we coped by leaning on each other in times of exceptional sadness and had we not been functioning in a multidisciplinary way perhaps we would have had to resort to the less satisfactory way of opting out. For example, we could have been very factual, giving the painful news in medical terms and being as brief as possible. We could have avoided the parents once they had been told or we could have arranged for them to have tranquillizers to dampen down their grief. But we knew that in the long term this was not likely to be helpful to the parents, and that we should not protect our own feelings by not getting involved with theirs. It was important for the team to remain serene and for the social worker, in particular, to listen to and to bear the repetition of the parents' reactions to their grief as many times as was necessary for the healing process, to tolerate their anguish with empathy and without ever prematurely cutting it off. We supported their expression of feelings and reassured them that it was normal. We encouraged them to regard it as a period of convalescence to an illness that would probably take at least a month and often longer to begin to recede. The social work continued until the mourning period seemed to be over and the emotional equilibrium was well along towards restoration. The death of the child was never seen as the end of the episode.

The actual telling of the parents was planned very much according to the findings of the survey. Our practice was to see the parents as a team and for the consultant to give the medical information, with perhaps a few comments from the junior doctor and from me. Then I would stay on with the parents, allowing them to grieve and sharing the sadness with them. It was very much a time of being on hand, being readily available and giving fairly basic tea and sympathy. Some twelve to twenty-four hours later it was anticipated that the parents would be ready for a longer interview in which there would be much more discussion of the implications of the condition, perhaps a need to recognize that their baby was a person and not a thing, that he or she needed a name and a place as a member of their family. As a team we tried to liaise closely and if there was any further important information to be given the consultant would try to do it when I was with him.

It took some time for the referral procedure to get established and for the consultants and registrars to move to a new pattern of working, which was to call the social worker in at the very beginning and in *every* situation, not just those where parents appeared to be incapacitated by the information and where the social worker was needed to try to help pick up the pieces. It was very much an experiment of giving social work help intensively at the moment of crisis, and when movement forward and continuing progress was seen to be made, the social worker would withdraw. The follow-up interview done in most cases a month or so later was principally to see that the mourning process was proceeding in a healthy way and that no further involvement was necessary.

> *Calm, calm me more! nor let me die*
> *Before I have begun to live.*
>
> MATTHEW ARNOLD

Ten of the children referred to me during my time at the hospital died, nine in the neonatal or immediate post neonatal period and one at the age of two. Had these children lived it is probable that they would have been severely handicapped. However, the main reason for the referral was that these children were likely to die. One mother (Mrs Cooper) was seen after her baby had died at two hours old; all the other mothers were seen first while their babies were still alive. The mother whose baby died so soon after delivery was not referred until two days later, just as she was about to go home. She was well sedated, still upset, but very anxious to get home where she had a good family network of support. The referral was rather too late for social work intervention to be meaningful and it was appropriate to acknowledge this. Similarly one case (the Old family) was transferred from a social work colleague who had had to take leave unexpectedly and it was rather late for either social worker to attempt to achieve much. The baby was an exceedingly small and very premature infant who hung on to life for five weeks. The stress of this considerably aggravated existing marital disharmony. I saw both parents separately; then the father had to be away for a week and the baby died before any work could be done. Each parent was angry with the hospital. They disagreed with each other about consent for a post-mortem so one could not be carried out, and refused to have any further contact with the doctors or the social worker. The professionals thought their help was needed but recognized the parents' right to refuse.

Of the remaining eight cases the referrals were all well timed. In seven cases the consultant involved discussed with the social worker his medical concern for the child; together it was agreed how and when to tell the parents, and in all cases this was done jointly. In the eighth situation the baby was a bad spina bifida. The parents had noticed at the delivery and had had to be given some information immediately. It is this case which I use as the second illustration. The first is also a baby born with a spina bifida. All names are pseudonyms.

## ALLEN FAMILY

Mr and Mrs Allen were a young couple in their early twenties who were living temporarily in the city for two years while Mr Allen completed a naval posting. It was their first pregnancy.

### Day 2

Mrs Allen delivered of a baby daughter at 9:30 p.m. last night. The baby had a severe spina bifida, and the mother was told that no active treatment would be undertaken beyond making the baby comfortable. Dr Brown telephoned me at home first thing this morning and we saw Mr and Mrs Allen together on the ward at 10 a.m. Dr Brown explained clearly and as simply as possible what a spina bifida was and why it was incompatible with normal life. The baby had had some clear fluid and some sedation and was comfortable. How long she would live he did not know.

Mr Allen was visibly much more upset than his wife was, who kept saying that it just had not hit her yet. He said very little during the interview and sat looking at his hands quite a lot, but at one point he did take hold of his wife's hand. It was then that he said they were glad that the baby was so badly deformed that she would not live because they would not have been able to manage a handicapped child. They took up our suggestion that we all go up to the Special Care Baby Unit and we helped Mrs Allen out of bed and took her up in a wheel chair. At first they thought the baby looked very sweet lying there but when they drew back the covers and saw the extent of the deformity they were shattered. There was a large raw looking sac extending along the baby's back, and because the covering of neuroepithelium was thin and transparent they felt that they were looking at the inside of the baby. They put their arms around each other and leaned over the cot looking closely at the lesion, then they quickly covered it up with the sheet and came out of the cubicle and stripped off their gowns and masks.

Back in the ward they were able to talk much more freely with me of their feelings about first 'knowing' and then being told that something was wrong, about their wish to start another pregnancy as soon as possible and about wanting to go home to Wolverhampton immediately. Mrs Allen is to be discharged tomorrow and I said that I would see her before she went and we would decide what, if any, further social work help was needed.

## Day 3

I spoke with Sister on the obstetric ward before I saw Mrs Allen. She told me that she had spoken fairly bluntly to Mrs Allen because she regarded her plan to take an early discharge in order to travel to her old home as dangerous and irresponsible. Sister was afraid that Mrs Allen would be putting her own life at risk, and she expressed the view to me, that the Allens were an immature couple who needed to grow up and act more responsibly. Her impatience with this couple may well have been exacerbated by the stress she had been under recently. As often seems to happen after months when everything goes really well, there had been a spate of misfortune in the delivery room. The birth of two handicapped babies had been followed the next day by a stillbirth and the atmosphere on the ward inevitably was tense. Sister was absolutely right in her obstetric judgement on the wisdom of travelling in the ten days following delivery; her brusque manner may well have been her way of coping with all the feelings of tension, distress and failure that were around during this brief run of abnormalities. I promised her that I would discuss it with Mrs Allen.

When I went in to see Mrs Allen she was feeling not only the baby's loss but also the impact of Sister's comments perhaps more strongly than was warranted. She was very upset and wept throughout the interview. She was going home at lunch time and it had been arranged that the district midwife would be going in for the next eight days. After that, she had decided, they would be able to go to Wolverhampton only for a long week-end. We talked about the necessity of resting after having a baby and about the importance of having the support of their own family which would help them face the sadness. She thought that one set of parents might visit them for a few days, which seemed a reasonable compromise. Mrs Allen talked and talked about the baby and was very undecided about whether or not she would be able to go and see her again. I said that that was something only she could decide but we would support her in whichever decision she did make. She was concerned about becoming attached to her, and I recognized this as a very real dilemma. There were two points of view, one being not to get involved so that one did not get attached, the other being to get to know the baby so that there was someone whom they could remember clearly and look back upon. We talked about the double mourning process that they were likely to go through. Mrs Allen said that she and her husband had grown much closer in the last thirty-six hours and her husband thought it was important that they should manage on their own. I agreed that if they both felt strong enough then this was right, but it was important also to be able to share grief and not to think that everyone expected them to be stoic. Perhaps this expectation stems from service life, which demands that men must be men and overt emotional reactions minimized. Earlier Mr Allen had been very upset but he did not feel that he could share his grief with his wife or with us.

## Day 5

I telephoned Mr and Mrs Allen as soon as I heard that the baby had died during the night. They had been up to the hospital very early in the morning to collect the death certificate. Both said how relieved they were that the agony of waiting for the death had not gone on too long. The baby was going to be cremated, and then her ashes would be taken to Wolverhampton and interred in the churchyard of the church where they were married. They knew that they would soon lose the ties they had with this area but would always have links with Wolverhampton and they wanted the baby to be part of this. We arranged that I would see them when they came up to the hospital to discuss the post mortem report, but if there was anything that they needed help with they would get in touch with me.

## Month later

Mr and Mrs Allen were seen by Dr Brown and me. We began by asking them how they were and they seemed a little surprised that we were concerned about them. Both said that they were well, but it was Mrs Allen who did most of the talking and throughout we felt that Mr Allen was keeping a tight control on how he really felt. They were able to discuss very fully with us the post-mortem report, genetic counselling, amniocentesis and their personal attitude towards termination of pregnancy. Mrs. Allen was much more comfortable in talking about the baby they had lost and in looking forward to the pregnancy they were hoping to start.

This couple moved a long way in a short period of time when they faced the twin crises of losing the normal baby they were expecting and then the abnormal baby who arrived. Their baby did not live long, and they coped by not getting involved with her. Their marital relationship appeared to burgeon in the stress and it was this which enabled them to look forward so positively. I now believe that we did not intervene soon enough with this family and had the consultant and I spoken with the parents within an hour or so of delivery we would have been possibly of more help to this father. As it was he knew for twelve hours that something was wrong, even if he did not know how wrong, and by the time we saw him his defences were up. We missed the moment of malleability and openness to professional intervention; he had begun the adjustment process in his own way, which was not to let himself think about it too much. In the short term this may be effective but it delays the process of facing what has to be faced, coming to terms with it and letting the wound heal in a healthy way. Mrs Allen had a delayed initial reaction and because of this we were around and very available at her crisis point and were able to offer her appropriate help. In our last interview with them Mrs Allen appeared to be better adjusted. We thought that Mr Allen was still suffering, but was sustained by the quality of their relationship with each other.

## WILLIAMS FAMILY

This was a young couple who had both lived in the city all their lives. Mr Williams had recently been made redundant.

### Day 1

The paediatric registrar rang me at home. Baby Williams had been born that afternoon and was a bad spina bifida who would be allowed to die. The consultant on call for the weekend was not coming in but the houseman was going to speak with the parents that evening. I arranged to join her, but when I arrived, she had had to speak with them earlier and did not want to go in again, so I saw them on my own. Both parents had seen the baby at delivery and were horrified. They knew that she would not live and did not want to have any contact with her. Although they were adamant that they did not want to go to the Special Care Baby Unit I thought that Mrs Williams wavered a little on this. I asked about names and baptism but Mr Williams said that they did not want either. Mrs Williams mentioned that previously she had had a spontaneous abortion and asked if it had been because the baby had been imperfect. Her husband was very quiet during the interview and at times did not seem to be listening to what his wife was saying. She had been booked in for eight days but very much wanted to go home, and this seemed to be the best thing for her. I spoke to Sister about this and she agreed that an early discharge would be possible. I arranged to see Mrs Williams again before she went home.

## Day 2

As I had to be out of the hospital during the day I rang early to find out when Mrs Williams was going home and was told that it would be tomorrow. I arranged to see her during the evening but when I went in she had already gone home!

## Day 5

I had a discussion with Sister on the Special Care Baby Unit. Mrs Williams had just telephoned and asked that the baby be baptized and had given a name. We arranged for the hospital chaplain to come in during the afternoon and do this.

In the late evening Baby Williams died. The houseman just missed me on the Intensive Care Unit, where I had been seeing some other parents, and I did not get the message until after 10 p.m. when I got home. I telephoned back to the hospital and spoke with the houseman. We decided that as it was so late I would go and see the parents first thing in the morning rather than upset them so late at night.

## Day 6

I called round at the home address but there was nobody in, and I was informed that they were with Mrs. Williams' mother. With some difficulty the address was traced later that day but in view of the delay and distance I telephoned. Mr Williams was out and his wife was in the bath, but Mrs Williams' mother seemed very helpful and perhaps it was better for her to give the news to her daughter. I said that I would ring back in 15 minutes and then I spoke with Mrs Williams. After talking about the death and making arrangements for them to come up for the Death Certificate, I gently mentioned the question of a post-mortem.

Later in the morning the registrar, the houseman and I saw Mr and and Mrs Williams. The registrar outlined the genetic factors and the risk ratio and they readily agreed to a post mortem. Again it was Mrs Williams who did most of the talking and she said that she had wanted to come up last night to see the baby but perhaps as things had turned out it was as well that she did not. I did not agree but did not say so. I believed that they might find it easier to mourn the loss of a child who had been 'real' to them, than one they had refused to know and Mrs Williams' behaviour suggested that she, at least, had mixed feelings about their decision. But they had chosen this course and, at this stage, it would have been no help to them to express my doubts. I stayed and spoke with the parents on their own. Mrs Williams cried and her husband was inclined to think that she should not be upset so I spoke about the need to grieve and that crying was a part of this. Mr Williams was under the impression that the hospital would do all that there had to be done and got quite cross when I explained that as it was a live birth the funeral arrangements were the responsibility of the family. He had not registered the birth and was not happy about having to go and do both. I took them down to see the clerk who handles the issue of death certificates and she explained to them what they had to do and that the cost would be about £15. Outside I told them that as Mr Williams was unemployed the Department of Health and Social Security would help with the financial side. Something seemed very wrong and I could not understand Mr Williams' extreme reaction. I offered to help them sort out the arrangements but Mrs Williams said that it was all right and they would go straight down to the Registrar's office.

## Two weeks later

Mr and Mrs Williams made an appointment to see the paediatric registrar. During this session Mr Williams told him that he had fathered a child in an earlier liaison who had been born with a very severe deformity, perhaps a spina bifida, and had died.

## Three weeks after that

I wrote a letter and suggested that I visit Mr and Mrs Williams at home. When I arrived I found that Mr Williams had gone to have tea with his mother so I only saw Mrs Williams and her sister-in-law, who wanted to discuss the risk of her having a deformed child. Mrs Williams was feeling much better and said she was hoping to get pregnant again very soon. She commented that she did not feel as if her previous pregnancy had come to an end because she could not remember the baby and added that for her the next one would be a case of third time lucky. I asked her how her husband was and she said that he was fine but he was not trying to get a job anymore because the wages he could earn were less than social security. They had sorted out the funeral information and the baby had been buried in a communal hospital grave.

There are several similarities between these two cases, yet they were to receive different types of professional care, and this may have contributed considerably to the different outcomes. Both babies were girls, first born children to young couples in their twenties and each was born with a severe spina bifida. Each child lived for five days, and the parents were seen within twelve hours of delivery by the social worker. But this is as far as the similarities go. In the first case the consultant and social worker spoke together before seeing the parents and did a planned joint interview. At no time in the second case did the consultant communicate with the social worker, nor see the parents. The houseman who spoke to these parents had had very little experience of giving bad news and chose to do this alone rather than as a member of a team. The social worker never really knew what medical information the parents had been given and what they had not heard. In due course these parents made further contact with the registrar to discuss Mr Williams' other baby, and this was an important breakthrough point, but it was not fully appreciated or communicated to the social worker until some time later. Obviously these parents had found their contact with this doctor helpful and more of it should have been offered to them. Mr and Mrs Allen arranged their baby's funeral, went to it and to the cremation, then took the ashes back to their place of origin. Mr and Mrs Williams did not have any ceremony in which they could take part and created no shrine to which they could return. The Allens had made contact with their baby after delivery; the Williams chose not to do so. The experience of the first couple was that their marriage had been strengthened but for the second couple the stress caused quite a lot of strain between them. For Mr Williams it was the third pregnancy with which he had been involved and as yet he had not proved that he could produce a normal child and it is fair to presume that this mattered very much to him. A lot of blame appears to have been projected, and the fact that he had no job and they lived in poor accommodation did not help. The social worker did little that was helpful to the Williams family. Even telling them that their baby had died was bungled, mostly due to faulty communication. The fact that Mr Williams went to tea with his mother when the social worker did the follow up visit is a fair assessment of his probable regard for the professional intervention. The Allen case illustrates good team work in facilitating the mourning process; the Williams case shows lack of team work, and little was done that was effective in enabling a healthy grief reaction.

## FIELD FAMILY

The third example is of a baby who lived for a very short while but whose parents were very involved with her during her brief life. There was good team work by the professionals involved.

### Day 1

The paediatric registrar telephoned me at home at 5 a.m. to say that a baby with gross abnormalities had been born and that the consultant Dr Jones was on his way in and had asked that I join him to see the parents. After examining the baby on the Special Care Baby Unit we went with the registrar and the houseman to the ward to see the parents. Mrs Field was fairly drousy and her husband, having been up all night, was very tired. Dr Jones catalogued the abnormalities (which included a cleft palate, extra digits, club feet and an inoperable heart condition) and explained what could and needed to be done. The parents were left with a reasonably positive picture of the situation. I stayed on for a brief while after the doctors had left and we talked about the possibility of there being other abnormalities which were not obvious at this stage. I arranged to see them the following morning when they had had a good sleep when we could begin to look at the situation and the implications for them of having a handicapped child. Both parents were too exhausted at this stage to think about anything much except needing to sleep.

### Day 2

The houseman telephoned me at 2 a.m. to say that Baby Field was giving rise to extreme concern. We discussed this but decided that unless death seemed imminent we should delay telling the parents until the morning. They had not slept the previous night and we thought they needed rest to face what the day ahead might hold for them. Perhaps the houseman and the social worker needed their rest as well. I said that I would be in first thing unless there was a marked deterioration, in which case I would go straight in. Next morning I joined the houseman and Dr Jones on the Special Care Baby Unit. Baby Field was on the ventilator but was extremely ill. It was now known that she was also blind, that unnecessary prolongation of life was not justified and that she should be allowed to die peacefully. The houseman and I went to see the parents. Mr Field had been sent for but had not arrived; Mrs Field was very upset. We spoke with her until her husband and his parents came in and then we let them have a little time on their own together before we spoke with Mr and Mrs Field. Earlier the baby had been baptized with Mrs Field present. The houseman very gently told them that their baby was not going to live and that she was going to be made comfortable and allowed to die in peace. They asked a few things about the deformities and whether she was suffering in any way and then we took them up to the unit to see her. We encouraged them to take her mittens off and to hold her hands. Both parents were very upset and wept freely as they stood there. When they felt that they had had enought we took them to join the grandparents in the ward sitting-room which was made available for this family's sole use. Although grandparents are usually only allowed to view from the window Sister gave her permission for both lots of grandparents to come in separately to see the baby. I helped them to put on gowns and took them in. Only Mr Field's mother could bring herself to wash her hands and to take hold of the baby's hand but it was very important to her to do this. It was she who was looking after the couple's elder child and it was she and her husband who were able to be especially helpful to Mr and Mrs Field in this situation. They all stayed in the flat and I made them some tea.

Baby Field died at 11:05 a.m. Mr Field had just taken his parents home and although Mrs Field guessed what we had to tell her she did not want to hear anything until he had come back. I rang him at home and within ten minutes he was back in hospital. The houseman told them that the baby had just died. Mrs Field asked if she could see her. The nurses who had been 'specialling' the baby dressed her and we took the parents in. As they gazed at her we asked them if they would like to hold her. Mrs Field wanted to do this and we lifted the little body out of the cot, gave it to her and then left them to say their own farewells in private. When they came out of the cubicle Mr Field was in great distress but Mrs Field was calm. The opportunity to hold the baby was important and later she told me that this was the first time she had done so and it had mattered very much to her. There is evidence that the loss of a child who is real and 'known' (however briefly) gives grief a sharper focus, enabling the healing process of mourning to take place more naturally. We therefore talked about the need to grieve and that part of this process was to have a memory upon which to focus. Although their baby had only lived for a day they had seen a lot of her in that time and would have something very tangible to recall. Agreement was readily given to a post-mortem being carried out and arrangements were made for Mrs Field to be discharged. Mr Field would come in the following day for the death certificate.

Three weeks later

Mr and Mrs Field came back to see Dr Jones and me to hear the post-mortem findings. In addition to the multiple abnormalities that were known to them there were chromosomal variations indicating that the baby was more male than female. Dr Jones suggested that there was so much wrong with this baby that it was perhaps the best thing that could have happened for her to die so soon after being born and they agreed. The odds against this happening again were about 100:1, but the parents agreed to have an appointment made with the geneticist and to be guided by her counselling. They had been away for a holiday with their little son and were feeling and looking much better. This couple adjusted well to their situation, mourned their loss and came through the experience seemingly stronger and perhaps better able to deal with life's traumas. They plan to have another pregnancy if the risk is as slight as Dr Jones thought it was, and although in the last pregnancy they said they had very much hoped for a daughter, in any future one they said all that mattered was that they had a normal baby.

## GREEN FAMILY

This was a case in which a lot of guilt feelings were aroused and these had to be worked through before the process of adjustment could be started.

Day 2

Dr Jones telephoned me about a young mother of twenty-two who had been admitted late last evening with an ante partum haemorrhage and had had a Caesarian section. Following an obstetric history of one stillborn, two spontaneous abortions and two live births it had been agreed that she should be sterilized and this had also been done at the same time. Mrs Green did not want a third son and when she came round and knew that this was what she had she was very angry and extremely upset, (an indication that counselling before sterilization should have been offered). The baby was not well and had been transferred to the Special Care Baby Unit.

I went to see Mrs Green, who was in a side ward on her own. Apart from being a bit sore she was feeling quite well. Although she had had such a vehement outburst last night she could remember very little of what had happened and spoke this morning of needing to be grateful that she had a live baby after previously having lost three. She would have liked to have had a little girl and knew that she would hever have one now, but she was glad to have a Keith to add to her Kevin and Kenneth. Dr Jones joined us and told her that her baby was still poorly and needing respiratory help, but that his condition was such that active measures to save him at this stage were justified. The impact of this information on Mrs Green was quite considerable. It was the first time that any indication had been given to her that Keith might not live and the third son she had not wanted suddenly became very precious to her. She spoke of wanting to care for him and said that no matter how weak he was she would be able to manage. The Council had just allocated a bigger flat to them and although she said it was in a rough block her husband would decorate it right through and make it comfortable for them. Her mother lived nearby and would lend a hand with the other two little boys and she would give her attention to this one. Mrs Green was hanging on to the practical details of life, perhaps as a way of coping with the emotional impact of the news with which she had suddenly been faced.

Day 3

Mrs Green had been moved into a four bedded ward, which was much better for her because she was a gregarious person. Keith was holding his own but still quite ill. Today Mrs Green said that if he was going to be a vegetable she would agree that it would not be right to keep him going, but otherwise she would manage to care for him and would devote herself to him no matter how he was. Mr Green had not been in to the hospital because she said he feels so uncomfortable in any hospital situation, but when I suggested that it might be a good thing for the consultant and me to see them both together she thought that it could be arranged for the next day. During this morning's interview she cried and we acknowledged that we did not expect her to be bright and brave all the time.

Later that day Keith had two further brain haemorrhages and Dr Jones decided that the time had come for active medical intervention to cease. He arranged for us both to see the parents at 8:45 p.m. Mrs Green's parents came in and Mr Green brought his sister to give him some support. We spoke with all the family. Dr Jones told them gently that the baby was deteriorating and that he thought the time had come to take him off the respirator and to let him die peacefully. There was immediate agreement and appreciation expressed of the care given. After Dr Jones had left I took Mr and Mrs Green up to the Special Care Baby Unit to see Keith. At the door Mr Green's courage deserted him and his wife had to go in without him. She remained very calm. Her parents went up next and then her sister-in-law said that she would like to see the baby. They all prevailed upon Mr Green to go up with her or else he would live to regret not having seen his baby. By now all the tubes had been disconnected and the end was near but the sight of Keith lying in a cot covered by a blanket was less traumatic than it had been on the respirator. Mr Green managed to go in and peep at his son but came out quickly and broke down and wept upon my shoulder. He did not want to back to the family until he had recovered and his sister and I stayed upstairs with him talking about the situation. When he felt better he went back to the family group and they waited and wept together until we told them that Keith had died at 9:40 p.m.

Day 4

Mrs Green was expressing milk for the other babies. She felt 'cool, calm and collected', she said, but recognized that it would not always be like this. She asked about the practical details of funeral arrangements and the death grant and wanted to keep the discussion very much at this level.

Day 5

The post-mortem report was shown to Mrs Green. The fact that Keith had had a brain haemorrhage was a vital factor in her cognitive acceptance that his death was probably a blessing. It was also the catalyst which enabled her to talk about how she had felt when she was told that she had not had the little girl that she so much wanted. She remembered almost hating him, but as the tears streamed down her face, she said she had not known then that there was anything wrong with him. We talked about her response to knowing that he was having problems with his breathing and how she wanted to do everything for him and let her mother help with the other two boys. She supposed that she was 'trying to make it up to him.' We talked about mourning loss and that part of her grieving was the loss by death of Keith, but that she had also lost forever the chance of having 'the baby daughter in frilly pants' she had always wanted. From this we went on to look at the stages that people went through in the mourning process and that it was quite normal to be angry, tense, depressed, and at times to feel a lot of hostility. Mrs Green had had a slight post-partum depression following an earlier pregnancy and was tremendously reassured that the feelings she had were those of a normal person in a grieving situation, and she was not necessarily going to slip into a psychotic state. She decided that she would let her milk dry up now, which could have reflected that she did not feel a need to recompense the world any more or continue to attone her guilt. She was to be discharged over the week-end and the funeral would be at the beginning of the next week.

Day 6

Mrs Green was preparing to go home. During the last week she had suffered much, but had achieved a great deal in terms of her personal development. The little boys had been in to see her and she had told them that the new baby had gone to Jesus. They were young enough to be quite accepting of this. She felt that her enjoyment of them would be greater than before, and with this new view of life she left hospital. We both agreed that the social work task had been completed, but she knew where to contact me if there was any further help I could give. She had a good relationship with her Health Visitor and was looking forward to seeing her again. Later I telephoned the Health Visitor and put her fully in the picture and she carried on from there.

In all these cases the parents knew from almost the beginning that their baby was abnormal and very early on they were told that the baby would not live for very long. As a result, they were able to engage in anticipatory mourning and much of the work of grieving had been done before the death had occurred. In another two cases the parents had babies and for the first forty-eight hours everything was believed to be normal. Then symptoms developed which gave rise to concern and the parents who had begun to bond to what they believed to be a normal child had to readjust to an impaired child and then to a condition that was terminal. They needed much more professional help in the process of adjustment.

## THOMPSON FAMILY

This couple had a three-year-old son, and this was their second baby. They were both in their early twenties and lived with Mr Thompson's mother. Michael Thompson was transferred from the local maternity unit when he was two days old because he was vomiting. Dr Jones rang me at home and told me that the baby was going to have a laparotomy done at 4 p.m. and that he was going to see the parents at 3 p.m. When I got to the ward the medical team was having difficulty in getting the drip up and the parents were waiting. I spoke briefly to them and explained why so many people seemed to be rushing around. The anaesthetist rang from theatre to know why the baby was late in going down. Despite the delay we made an opportunity for the parents to see their baby and to touch him before he went down for the operation.

While Michael was in theatre Dr Jones and I spoke with the parents. He explained why it was necessary to do the operation and that it would enable a firm diagnosis to be made. He thought that in about half an hour there would be some information. I stayed and spoke with the parents. Mrs Thompson was concerned but calm; Mr Thompson was so tired after being on a night shift that he stretched out in the arm chair and went to sleep. While he slept Mrs Thompson spoke about living with her mother-in-law. She said that they had tried for numerous flats, but that nobody wanted children, even if there is only one. They are on the housing list but have not enough points yet to stand any chance of being allocated a house. Mr Thompson was unemployed for about a year and then got his present job, which entails doing four night shifts and then four day shifts; his sleeping routine is irregular. When Mrs Thompson was working she was responsible for the catering section in a large store. She was earning twice as much money as her husband, and this he found very difficult. She is perhaps the more intelligent of the two.

After much longer than half an hour Dr Jones came back from theatre with the news that part of Michael's gut had been removed and a temporary colostomy formed. There was still uncertainty about the baby's condition and he thought that there would be two fairly stormy days ahead. Next day Mrs Thompson went home and Mr Thompson came in each day to see the baby until his wife was allowed to visit. On the seventh day Michael needed further surgery and on the tenth day it was known that he had a rare form of Hirschsprung's disease affecting the whole bowel and that he would not live very long. Dr Jones told Mrs Thompson when she came to the ward to visit and I later went to see both parents at home. They were quiet and near to tears. Mrs Thompson did most of the talking; she had grasped very clearly the medical details and the implications for the future. Mr Thompson had been to register the baby's birth that morning before they had been told the bad news, and he now found this very distressing to think about. We spent a long time talking about why the baby would die and how much more difficult it was to face this when for more than a week they had believed that once he got over the operation for the blockage Michael would be all right. They said that they would not like to be given the news that he had died over the telephone and were grateful to know that I would go round to their house and tell them myself. I raised the question of baptism. Although they had not had their elder son baptized, they were keen for Michael to be done and said they would both like to be present. I found out the times which would be convenient for them and later telephoned the hospital chaplain and arranged that it should be done on Saturday morning. I went to get the parents so that they did not have to come up on the bus and after the brief ceremony took them home again.

Michael had been dressed in a special gown, bootees and bonnet by the nurses who had been looking after him and he looked very sweet. While we waited for the chaplain to come I encouraged them to take Michael out of the cot and to hold him, which Mr Thompson had not yet done. When the chaplain came he suggested that Mr Thompson sit and held Michael on his knee for the baptism. He explained to the parents what he was going to do and then with two of the nurses and me present as well he proceeded with a simple and moving ceremony. Afterwards we left the parents to cuddle and talk to Michael and then when they were ready we left the ward. On the way home Mr Thompson said that he felt a lot better about the whole thing. It had been very important to him to have held Michael and to have been asked to name the child because he felt that he had done something for his son.

Another week was to pass before Michael died. He gradually deteriorated but kept rallying a little, which was difficult for the parents and for the nurses. His parents continued to visit and to have contact with the social worker and the doctors. At 9:20 a.m. on Sunday morning I had a message from the hospital to say that Michael had just died, and I went straight round to see the parents. Mrs Thompson was upstairs dressing her elder son and saw me approaching. By the time she opened the front door there were tears in her eyes because she knew why I had come. Mr Thompson was at work, but she said that she would not ring him because it would upset him and she was worried that he would not be able to concentrate on the machinery on which he was working. We talked about the death certificate, making the funeral arrangements and the genetic counselling she had been promised. Nobody had yet mentioned doing a post-mortem but it was almost certain that Dr Jones would want to do this and he would want to see the parents to ask their permission. I promised to check this for her and to telephone her neighbour with any messages.

Dr Jones and I saw them together at the hospital in the evening. They were very agreeable to a post-mortem being done and asked about the risks of the same thing happening again if they were to have any more babies. Dr Jones explained that the post-mortem would help with this because it would confirm the diagnosis, but it was likely that the risk was quite high. When I took them home they talked about Michael and the range of opinions that well meaning friends and relatives had thrust upon them concerning future pregnancies. I stressed that the decisions were theirs, that all the doctors would do would be to give them the odds against its happening again, but would not advise them about the decision they took based on the odds. When we got to their home I said that although Michael had died, it did not mean that we had lost interest in them as a family. If there was anything we could do to help them we would be only too glad to do so. In any case I would see them to discuss the post-mortem report. As they got out of the car they thanked me for 'the wonderful support', yet at the time I was thinking how much this couple had achieved for themselves. They had coped most maturely with a difficult and harrowing experience.

The post-mortem report confirmed the original diagnosis and was sent to Great Ormond Street Hospital in London for expert comment. Mr and Mrs Thompson were seen about a month later and given the very high odds of 1:4 of this happening again. Both felt that the risk was too great and they planned not to have any more babies. They said they felt about ten years older but were looking forward realistically. Now that their little boy had started going to playgroup Mrs Thompson planned to go back to work so that they could start saving up to buy a place of their own.

## HARRIS FAMILY

This was a young couple with their first baby. For the first two days of the baby's life everything had seemed fine. The case was noteable for the extreme grief reaction exhibited by both parents and for much longer than is usual.

### Day 3

I was up on the ward early, having been called in to see another baby. Tracy Harris had been transferred to the Special Care Baby Unit because her temperature was slightly below normal and her respiratory rate was slightly raised. Although it was not yet 6 a.m., Mrs Harris was sitting outside the ward waiting for news. Dr Jones told her that he had examined the baby and thought that there might be some heart condition, but at the moment there was no cause for alarm. Mrs Harris was crying and when I stayed to talk with her she asked me if the baby was going to die. I replied that there was always some risk with new born babies, especially if a heart condition was suspected, but at the moment Dr Jones was feeling positive about the situation. She came with me to see the baby but was too upset to stay so I took her back to her ward and helped her get back into bed. Mr Harris came in soon afterwards; he looked briefly at the baby, listened to what Dr Jones had to say but did not ask any questions and went down to be with his wife. About an hour later I called in to that ward to see them and found them weeping together in great distress, so much so that the other mother who had been in that side ward had had to be moved out because she could not stand the weeping any more. Mrs Harris was sure that her baby would be a cabbage and she said that she would rather she died now than had to live like that. Apparently Mr Harris' niece had been born with a spina bifida so they have strong reactions and feelings about abnormalities and especially about anything mental. I talked about the possible effects of a heart condition but stressed that the brain should not be affected. Mr Harris said very little and this mostly to his wife. We had at this stage no firm diagnosis about the baby, yet they had virtually written her off. The bed was littered with damp lilac tissues and there seemed no way of assuaging their almost premature grief. We discussed the possibility of Tracy having to be transferred to one of the London hospitals that specialised in heart conditions, and this seemed to aggravate the situation. I arranged to see them again in the morning but I came away feeling that this grief reaction far exceeded what could be considered appropriate to the information given.

I had just got home at 8:10 a.m. when the houseman rang me to say that there had been a sudden and dramatic deterioration in Tracy's condition and that he thought she might be going to die. I went straight back to the hospital, and he and I went to see the parents. They were still crying. The houseman told them that their baby had become very ill, whereupon both parents began to wail and Mr Harris climbed up on to the bed and clung to his wife. We waited quietly. When things calmed momentarily we asked them if they would like to have their baby baptized. Mrs Harris said they would, but they did not think they could face being there. It would have been very difficult to get a priest at that time on a Sunday morning and so it was arranged for Sister to do a lay baptism. As the situation seemed to be urgent Sister went ahead and performed the simple ceremony; then the parents changed their minds and said they would like to be at their baby's baptism. Sister, with some concern, agreed to do it again. These parents were beginning to show a need for ritual and if we were to help them with their mourning it was important that this need be met.

Mr and Mrs Harris never knew that their baby had two baptisms but for those who attended both the ceremonies were equally dignified and moving. The parents at the second one each held one of the baby's feet and clung to each other in tears. Then they went into the flat and I made them a cup of tea. I spent some time with them and Mrs Harris asked several questions about Tracy but kept saying that there would be no more babies, she could not go through this again; whilst her husband tried to convince her that it was far too soon to make such decisions. None of the drugs was working and the baby's condition became critical. I went back to the parents and told them this, and asked them if they wanted to see their baby again or to remember her

as she was. They both wanted to come back to the ward and in fact
decided to stay with her to the end. We put two chairs near to the
incubator, and although the intermittent weeping continued they
were beginning to cope a little. I thought that any further intervention
at this stage would be an intrusion on their personal grief, so I told
them that I was going home but that the houseman would be around
all day and would see them at any time. They did not think there was
anything that anyone could do for them at that time. I said that I
would see them the following day. Tracy died at 2:30 p.m. and her
parents were able to stay with her to the end. Mrs Harris was immediately discharged from hospital and an arrangement made for Mr
Harris to come in next day to collect the death certificate and to see
Dr Jones and me.

### Day 4

Mr Harris came in with his father-in-law. Dr Jones asked for permission
to do a post-mortem but Mr Harris was very unhappy about this. Dr
Jones explained that it was requested so that as much information as
possible was made available to them in order to know the odds against
this happening again. However we were not putting any pressure on
them to agree to this being done, and his decision would be respected.
His father-in-law argued with him that if he did not agree the chance
of knowing what was wrong would be lost for ever and that he owed it
to his wife at least. Mr Harris did not really need much persuading; it
was just that he did not feel like making any decisions and was quite
glad for his father-in-law to decide for him. Mr Harris was still weepy
and did not want to talk.

### Three weeks later

Mr and Mrs Harris came early for their appointment with Dr Jones
and me which, unfortunately, had been made in the children's ward.
I was talking to some other parents on the ward but noticed that Mrs
Harris was looking distressed, so I went across. She was near to tears
and found being in the children's ward very upsetting, so I took them
out and Dr Jones and I saw them in the mothers' room. Dr Jones told
them that the baby had had only one ventricle in her heart and so had
not been able to sort and pump the blood. The odds against this happening again were about 200:1. Mrs Harris wept through most of the
interview; her husband kept putting his arm round her, holding her

hand, kissing her and doing his best to comfort her.

Mr Harris was back at work and said that this was a good thing because he forgot the domestic problems when he was with his work-mates. He is doing a labouring job at the moment, which means that he gets physically very tired and is able to sleep. His wife, on the other hand, is at home on her own all day. She gave up her job in anticipation of full time motherhood and now has very little to occupy her time and her thoughts. She felt angry with her family doctor, who had prescribed anti-depressants which she said had not done her any good at all – she had soon given up taking them. After a long interview Dr Jones and I both thought that I should do some more work with this couple. Mr Harris thought that his wife needed something but she said she would try to get over it. In the end she seemed quite happy for me to see her in a month when she thought she would be over it. Meantime we en-couraged her to think about work again and for them both to plan a holiday.

## Month later

I wrote to them and arranged to call and see them one evening after work. Mrs Harris was in tears before her husband had come down from the shower he was taking. She cried herself to sleep most nights, has a bad time about breakfast time every day and finds that she is fre-quently and unpredictably suddenly overwhelmed with pangs of grief. Her husband rarely sees this because he is either asleep or has gone to work. He is on valium because he gets so tensed up but his wife is not taking anything. When Mr Harris joined us he did say that he had to watch every word he said to his wife because she was so prickly. This seemed to surprise her and cause more tears. He can not under-stand her need to avoid people and said that it was becoming ridiculous when they had to dodge into shops because she had seen somebody whom she thought that she knew. Mrs Harris is due to have her post-natal examination next week and I suggested that she speak to her doctor about her feelings. I explained the psychological necessity to mourn and the recuperation which could follow if the process followed its natural course. However, sometimes a depression was only partially reactive and it was important to have a clinical assessment of this. Mrs Harris has been able to get her old job back and will return to work after they have been away for their fortnight's holiday. She is now worrying because she has not had a period since the baby was born, so

I told her to discuss this with her doctor. We arranged that I should see Mrs Harris on her own at home when she had been to see her doctor.

Week later

I called to visit Mrs Harris at 10 a.m. as arranged. The house was immaculate as always, but there was quite a changed Mrs Harris. She and her husband had found that they could say things to each other in my presence which they had not seemed able to before, and this had continued since. Today she was able to talk freely about the baby's death and to discuss her feelings then and now. There were the odd tears in the eye but the uncontrollable weeping had ceased and she said that there had been very little of it in the last week. Her family doctor thought that she should have her holiday and go back to work and if then she still felt depressed she should go back and see him. He did not think that she would be pregnant and again suggested waiting for a while to see if her periods started. However, this had not really helped Mrs Harris, who is already anxious about the next pregnancy and is likely to worry for much longer than the nine months that she is pregnant. We talked about how distress sometimes affects the menstrual cycle and looked also at the fact that although she was anxious about becoming pregnant they were not taking any contraceptive precautions. She recognized that she did have very mixed feelings, wanting to have a baby but fearing that the baby might not be normal. I suggested that when she did become pregnant again it would be a good thing for the maternity social worker to be involved and Mrs Harris agreed. We reviewed the social work contact that she had had during this bereavement and I pointed out to her that I now realized that I had left too long between her discharge from hospital and making the next contact. Mrs Harris said that that was partly her fault because she kept thinking that she would soon feel all right again. We were agreed that the social work contact should now cease.

This mother took more than ten weeks to begin to recover from her loss and her husband nearly as long, although his grief was dampened down with librium and relieved by his return to work. The social work intervention should have been much more concentrated in the period immediately after her discharge from hospital. It was obvious from the beginning that these parents were going to find coping with their grief would be difficult and they should have been offered much more help at an earlier stage. Looking back at the situation, I can see only two factors that might have influenced the timing. One was the slight reluctance on the parents' part; and they, and we, may have been influenced by the knowledge that time itself is a great healer. The other was that we may have been guided by the more usual time span in resolving the crisis which we had encountered in our work with other parents, and were not sufficiently alert to the unusual aspects of this family situation. In the last two interviews Mrs Harris was able to use social work in a constructive way. She was reassured that she was not on the way to the local psychiatric hospital, but experiencing a normal grief reaction. She began to understand that at the end of it she should be as strong as she was before and probably much more mature.

The final example in this section is concerned with the death of a little boy aged two. He had never been ill in his life and then quite suddenly he was struck down with a particularly nasty type of viral meningitis from which he did not recover consciousness. He was the much adored younger son of a couple who lived for and enjoyed every minute they had with their children. He had grown up in a small community surrounded by numerous great aunts and uncles and his grandparents, and was known to nearly everybody who lived locally. The loss for these parents was harder than in any of the previous examples because they were losing so much more; not a brief relationship that had hardly had a chance to get going, but a much cherished one of two years standing. On the positive side these parents had two years of memories which the other parents lacked. It was a harrowing experience for the parents and their family, and also for the staff who were involved in caring during the crisis. It was very much a team involvement and the team needed the support of each other to give the maximum service to the whole family.

## RICHARD THORPE

### Day 1

About 5:30 a.m. Richard woke up and was sick and went back to sleep. His father gave him a drink before he went to work and his mother went in soon after 8 a.m. to give him another. At 8:30 a.m. she found him unconscious. She rang her husband at work and the family doctor, both of whom came immediately. The doctor, himself, drove

Richard and his mother straight into the hospital followed by Mr Thorpe in his own car. As soon as they reached the ward a lumbar puncture was done which confirmed the diagnosis. At 2 p.m. Richard stopped breathing and was moved from the children's ward into the Intensive Care Unit and put on a ventilator. The houseman rang me in my office and I went straight over and was introduced to the parents by the registrar. They were in the little sitting-room on the unit which had been made available exclusively for their use.

Both parents were prostrate with grief and could give very little support to each other. I began by asking them what the doctor had told them and they kept repeating that it was very serious and they did not want him to be a cabbage. Very gently I led them back over what had happened and they were able to keep going through the events of the morning and say how well he had been yesterday and described how he had sat on his father's knee to watch the European Cup Final last night. Amid all their tears Mrs Thorpe kept saying that she would never be able to watch football again and that he had had lovely clothes and that she had dressed him up every day. They talked about all the things he did and what he said. As their confidence in me seemed to grow they were able to ask about the outcome and acknowledge that the chances of Richard's surviving were remote.

Although the nursing staff were actively treating Richard I thought that it was important for these parents to have access as and when they needed. They found it difficult to go into the treatment room and at the beginning Mr Thorpe could do this only very briefly. We gave them a chair on each side of the bed and encouraged them to hold Richard's hands. Mrs Thorpe was able to do this but her husband could not stay near his son. An aunt and uncle who are very close to the family came in and stayed for a while in the sitting-room. They had organized the picking-up of the elder brother from school and one of the grannies was going to have him to stay for the night. They said that Mrs. Thorpe's mother had had hysterics when she had been told about Richard.

Dr Fergus came in to examine Richard and did not exclude the parents while he did so. Earlier the staff nurse had thought that she had got a slight response from the pupil, and the primitive response of the foot had been seen, but there was no evidence of this when Dr Fergus made his examination. He spoke with the parents and told them that there would be no change for twenty-four hours but that the situation remained very serious. We encouraged them in their wish to go home briefly. They were a bit worried about being in their working clothes and wanted to have a wash and change. We said that they could stay the night in hospital or come and go, whichever arrangement suited them best. As they left I suggested that they bring back Richard's teddy or the toy that he took to bed with him each night. The aunt and uncle briefly saw Richard but were too distressed to remain in the room with him. They were very supportive to the young couple.

I returned to the hospital just before 9 p.m. Mr and Mrs Thorpe were back and had brought a few things in for the night, as well as Richard's gollies, which were tucked up in bed with him. There was no change at all in his condition, but unfortunately the alarm bell on the ventilator was faulty. Its continual ringing caused the parents a lot of unnecessary anxiety. The anaesthetist came and checked it and sent the parents out. After he had fixed it I asked him if he would have a brief word with the parents and explain what had been wrong. He seemed surprised but did so, and they felt reassured that it had been a faulty connection. The night staff came in and introduced themselves to Mr and Mrs Thorpe, who were fairly calm by now and much reassured that some of the doctors slept in the hospital and were readily accessible. I told them if there was any deterioration in Richard's condition during the night I would come in, otherwise I would see them first thing in the morning.

## Day 2

I went to the Intensive Care Unit soon after 8 a.m. to be greeted by another Sister with, "If you're the social worker thank goodness you've come; they're in a terrible state." Although there was no change in Richard's condition there had been no improvement in the reflex patterns and the parents knew that he was not going to live. There had been a gap between the time they were told that he was unlikely to live and knowing this of about eighteen hours. They were very distressed again, going through another periodic weeping stage. They were saying that they would have to move away from their present home because they would not be able to tolerate seeing the other children who lived near them growing up. Mrs Thorpe could sit by Richard, but Mr Thorpe was hyperactive and could not settle anywhere. The nursing staff suggested that he go out of the hospital for a walk or that he sit down on a chair, but when I explained to them why he could not do either, they let him pace up and down the corridor and in and out of the room and he wished. It made the nursing less organized, but it helped a grieving father and the nurses when they understood this, could not have been more co-operative.

Dr Fergus came and after examining Richard told the parents that he planned to keep him on the ventilator for the time being and perhaps over the weekend. He was going to arrange for an electro-encephalogram to be done, which would show if there was any brain activity. Mr Thorpe pleaded with Dr Fergus not to let Richard live if he was going to be a cabbage and not to use him as a guinea pig. Dr Fergus listened sympathetically to him, but said that he would make the medical decisisions, and his decision at this stage was to continue treatment. We then talked about how we could help Mr and Mrs Thorpe with their personal agony. The houseman had given them some valium and had telephoned their family doctor, whom they knew well, to ensure that the medical care continued. We would give what emotional support we could at the hospital.

The aunt and uncle, two grannies and a grandad came in. Mrs Thorpe wept loud and long on her mother-in-law's shoulder. There is a good family network here because two brothers married two sisters and they are all very close. Mrs Thorpe's father died of cancer, so she has had some experience of losing a close relative, and it may explain why marginally she is coping better than her husband who, as yet, has never lost anyone whom he loved dearly. I made tea for the family and served it to them. Then, with the exception of the maternal grandmother, who is inclined to faint and have hysterics, each one went in to see Richard. They were all very upset but were glad that they had been able to bring themselves to do this. It was agreed the best thing would be for the parents to go home for a break. They understood that life was being maintained artificially and that there could be no change while this was being done. We encouraged them to telephone in as many times as they wished.

Soon after 2 p.m. Dr Fergus had the results of the electro-encephalogram, which showed that there was no brain activity at all and he decided that it was futile to proceed with treatment. The parents had not returned, nor telephoned, but rather than send the police to find them and by so doing alarm them, we agreed to wait until they came back in. I thought they would probably meet their other son from school and then return, and this in fact was what they did.

Dr Fergus and I saw them together. He told them that there was no brain activity and no hope for Richard and asked them if they would wish the ventilator to be turned off. Mr Thorpe became very calm at this stage and persuaded his wife to agree. Dr Fergus went out for a while and we spoke about the situation. Mrs Thorpe asked if she could hold Richard and I went to ask Dr Fergus who agreed. I took her back into the treatment room and helped her sit down by the bed. Richard, still with numerous tubes attached to him, was lifted onto her knee. As she hugged him to her the ventilator was switched off and he died in her arms. Both parents kissed him good-bye and when they were ready we took them out of the room. Mrs Thorpe went to her uncle and Mr Thorpe had a long talk with Dr Fergus. Somebody gave him a drink, which was probably not a good thing, because he did not usually drink. A calmness began to descend and we made arrangements for the immediate issue of the death certificate so that they did not have to come back into the hospital again. Mr Thorpe did not seem to want to be with his wife and appeared to need the routine administrative tasks as an outlet for his hyperactivity. Mrs Thorpe desperately wanted to get away and I suggested that her uncle took her home and that I brought her husband when everything was tied up, but she insisted on waiting for him. He seemed to be reluctant to leave the place. Finally I had to say to him that his wife really did need to go, so he drank the brandy straight back, collected Richard's clothes and gollies and the death certificate and went to her. Through their tears they said good-bye to the registrar and me and said that they knew everything that could have been done had been done. We, who were left, blinked away our own tears, talked about the tragedy and watched a shrouded bundle leave the Intensive Care Unit for the mortuary.

## Month later

This was a long interview, but it was perhaps the first time since Richard had died that Mr and Mrs Thorpe had talked at length about it. Their other son was still up when I got there but after a little chat with me he went off to bed. He is waking up in the night and complains of aches in the throat, arm, teeth and tummy much more than he ever did before. I explained to his parents why this might be and how children of his age (nearly 6) had little understanding of death and the finality of it, but that going to sleep sometimes brought with it separation anxieties and he may have fears that this might be what happened to Richard.

Mr and Mrs Thorpe had a very real need to talk and at times could hardly wait for the other to finish before adding something. They went through the events leading up to Richard's death, the days that followed, the funeral, the cremation and the problems with people being uncomfortable and not knowing what to say. The families had rallied round them; Mrs Thorpe's mother had come to stay for a while and done all the cooking because all they had felt like doing was to sit in a chair. They soon stopped taking the tablets because they had made them feel drousy and they thought that they began to feel better after that. Last week they had been to Cornwall for the holiday for which they had already booked and paid. They went without enthusiasm and mostly for their son's sake and did not particularly enjoy it, but it had been a change and an attempt to keep going.

Early in the interview Mrs Thorpe cried a little and her husband looked anxiously at her, but let her be, knowing that there was still a need to cry and that it was part of the process of mourning in which they were both engaged. She also smiled during the interview and was able to look forwards as well as backwards. Originally Mr Thorpe had thought two children was enough, although his wife had wanted a third and had hoped for a girl. Now they were beginning to talk about having two more babies because their son would be so much older than any subsequent children they might have. Mrs Thorpe is 31 and it took a year to conceive Richard so she is a little worried about managing to start a pregnancy but knows that there is plenty of time.

This couple have moved a long way in a month and are realistically facing up to a new and at the moment much more empty life. All of Richard's toys and clothes have been put away and his photograph removed from the sideboard. We talked about this and the necessity of having done it now, but that in the future it should go back in its place. Richard was part of their family and his memory needed to be preserved and his former presence acknowledged. They will be able to do this in time. They know that part of them died with him, but they also grew together as a couple and developed strengths within themselves which have enabled them to stay in their present house, to mix with other families again and even to go to the street Jubilee party a few days after the funeral. Life will not be the same for them but they are taking a positive look to the future and all augurs well for them. I offered to sort out some minor problems about the death certificate which I did next day. They were appreciative of the help and care which they had had from the hospital and Mrs Thorpe said that she would be able to face going back there to have any other babies. At this stage I raised the point of not being able to replace but only add to a family's membership. Another baby would not take Richard's place; it would be a baby in his own right as he had been. I believe they were already understanding this because Mrs Thorpe said that perhaps it would be better if a girl arrived next although it was a boy dominated family.

We agreed that if there were times in the future when they felt the hospital may be able to help them they would make contact with us, but at the moment they were making a good recovery and the case should be closed. Two months later I received a letter to let me know that Mrs Thorpe was pregnant and they were all absolutely delighted. She would be having her baby in the hospital and did not mind coming back at all now.

*How long does the fire of love endure*
*If the eyes and touch are not there to kindle it?*
DANTE: THE DIVINE COMEDY

The timing of telling parents that their child is handicapped and expected to live could not be more controversial. There has been a considerable amount of work done on the effects of very early separation of babies from their mothers (Klaus, Kennell and Whiten) which suggests that for a non-specific time after birth there is a period of heightened sensitivity for the mother—child bonding process. Not only may separation be detrimental to this process but also factors such as whether the baby is small, sick or handicapped may influence the relationship. It could be argued that if the parents are told during this period of heightened sensitivity that there is something wrong with their baby, the bonding process could be impaired as a direct result. However against this is equally good evidence (Stokes) that acceptance is more readily possible when the diagnosis is given early in a child's life. Certainly there was a strong plea from the parents whom I interviewed in the survey for parents to be given information early. I believe it is important to be honest with parents, and that they must have all the information that is available so that they know to whom they are, or are not, bonding. We planned, therefore, that as soon as we knew that a child could be handicapped we should see the parents jointly and share with them our concern.

Many of the problems stem from the medical necessity of entering the baby into a Special Care Baby Unit and separating it from the mother. Although she is encouraged to be involved with her baby's care, the skilled nursing care that is required often makes the contact minimal and not meaningful. The mother is not handling her baby, feeding him or just looking at him. Although a baby may be saved, there is a slight risk that a mother may be lost. The social worker's help in achieving a balance is important here, as is his guidance on the timing of giving parents any information.

Four of the babies with definitely diagnosed long-term handicaps were born with Down's syndrome. Three were clinically obvious and the parents were told within the first twenty-four hours; with the fourth there was some uncertainty and it was the third day before the information was given to the parents. In two cases confusion and non-acceptance initially abounded and one parent in each situation had particular difficulty in facing the outcome. Inevitably when a mother is more continuously concerned with looking after a child, it is perhaps harder for the family when it is she who struggles longer and finds the move towards acceptance so tortuous. The first example is of such a situation and unfortunately it was this mother whom the consultant first told on her own that he thought there might be something wrong with her baby.

## CANN FAMILY

### Day 1

Dr Fergus spoke with Mrs Cann soon after she was delivered of her third child and first daughter. He told her that the baby had some characteristic features of Down's syndrome and that he would like to discuss it with her and her husband the following day. When she told her husband at visiting time both were very upset, but the houseman was the only member of the team available and he did not know what information the consultant wished them to have. All he could do was to try to contain the situation until the next day. Understandably, the parents were angry when Dr Fergus and I went to see them.

### Day 2

Dr Fergus repeated the information that he had given to Mrs Cann and perhaps because there was so much mixed emotion in the situation, he tended towards taking a very clinical approach, focusing on a scientific exploration of the occurrence of Down's syndrome. Mrs Cann did not say a word throughout the interview, and all the questions came from her husband. Both seemed dazed. After asking a few basic details, Mr Cann said that he thought they had taken it as far as they could at that moment and that he was too stunned to think of any more things that they would need to know. After Dr Fergus had left I stayed and spoke to them about family life with a child who had Down's syndrome but it was not the right time for them to discuss it. They were far too overcome with the information to try to cope with interpreting it into their personal situation. Mrs Cann had not been able to cry and remained silent but gave the odd sad half smile. She was only booked in for a forty-eight hour delivery, so I suggested that I telephone them at home in a week's time and if they would like me to I would come and see them at home.

A week later

I telephoned the parents and spoke to Mr Cann, who was still on holiday. He told me that his wife was not accepting the situation, did not want to talk about it and until that morning had not been able to express any grief. He was keen for me to go round but he said that he would have to talk to his wife and ring me back. Two days later he telephoned and we arranged one evening in the following week. On the morning of the planned visit Mr Cann telephoned me from work to say that he was concerned about his wife's continuing non-acceptance of the situation and asked me not to give a black picture when I called that evening.

Home visit. It was 8 p.m. and the two sons and new baby Paula were in bed. Mr and Mrs Cann were sitting together waiting for me. As Mrs Cann had not said anything in the previous interview, I tried to focus on her at the beginning of this one, but Mr Cann always seems to be the spokesman for the marriage and he quickly took over his familiar role. We discussed aspects of Down's syndrome generally, the need for special education and the facilities for this within the area. I mentioned the financial provision made for handicapped children and their families. Although Mr Cann said that he had an uncomfortable feeling of cashing in on handicap he acknowledged that there could be additional expense in caring for Paula.

When we looked back to their being told of Paula's condition

Mr Cann was still angry about his wife being given the information on her own and said that this should not have been done. I agreed with him and said that our more usual practice was to wait until both parents were together and what had happened had been especially hard for Mrs Cann. Later when Paula was due for a feed her mother brought her down. While she gave her a bottle Mr Cann went to make some tea. It gave me a brief opportunity to speak with Mrs Cann on her own. She said that she was very saddened by the situation and could only cope by keeping it bottled up inside her. I spoke a little about mourning the loss of the normal baby she had been expecting and how much more difficult it must have been to accept the abnormal daughter who had arrived instead. When Mr Cann joined us he picked this up. Both sons were at shcool now and they had debated long as to whether or not to have another child. Now that they had a handicapped child it made some of their earlier ambivalent feelings that much stronger. He spoke warmly about the importance of Mrs Cann in their family unit and how they needed her not to be strained but enjoying life with them all again. This was perhaps the most useful part of the session and in it Mrs Cann moved a little way towards the acceptance of their life as it now was likely to be. I recognised with them that this would be gradual and might not necessarily every be achieved totally. If Mrs Cann felt that she could only continue to function by keeping her feelings to herself then we should support her in this for the time being, but be available to her if, and when she felt differently. She gets much support from her husband, and this was a very important element in the process at this stage.

Time has shown that the giving of information to this mother without her husband's support was almost destructive of the situation and she walked a tight rope between acceptance and non-acceptance of this baby for a long time. Several weeks later this was still a fragile area. This might have been so however they were told, but when it is known that telling parents early and together makes for better acceptance, situations should not be put at risk by deviation from this practice.

The second case was of a baby boy whose condition was not so clinically obvious and whose parents did not suspect that anything was amiss. Because he was slightly premature, he was in the Special Care Baby Unit, so there was some separation from mother. However, she was keen to breast feed and was expressing milk and being as involved as she could at this stage. There was very much a planned team involvement in the telling of the parents and the subsequent care of this family and I believe we got the process as near to right as we ever did. I quote in detail this as an example, perhaps even a model of how to handle telling parents of their child's handicap when some little time has elapsed between birth and the event.

## STEPHENS FAMILY

Dr Brown came to see me about 4 p.m. Baby Stephens was born two days ago about three and a half weeks premature. The houseman had thought that there was some indication of Down's syndrome but Dr Brown when he saw the baby was not sure and had asked the registrar who had specialized knowledge in this area also to examine him. The registrar had just done this. They were almost certain that the baby was a Down's syndrome and had sent blood off to Bristol for confirmation. The question was when to tell the parents. Should we tell them now while there was some doubt or should be wait until the results came back from Bristol. I had no doubts about this and possibly pressed for telling as soon as we could organize a joint meeting with the parents. After checking with the ward that Mr Stephens would be visiting his wife that evening we arranged to see the parents together at 8 p.m.

### Day 3

Mr and Mrs Stephens came up to the Special Care Baby Unit a little before the time arranged and immediately said that they were very worried about having to see the paediatric consultant. Unfortunately Dr Brown was delayed and all I could do was to recognise the anxiety with them and say that any medical information had to come from the consultant. (In a perfect situation it might have been preferable for the parents not to have any prior warning that the consultant wished to see them and somehow he should be passing — with the social worker — when the father just happened to be visiting his wife. This is not to deny the functional value of anxiety but we gave them absolutely nothing on which to focus their anxiety. Perhaps at 4 p.m. we could have told Sister arranging the meeting to say that although Peter was very well there were one or two features which might make for problems in the future and that we would like to discuss these with them.)

Dr Brown and the houseman joined us. Dr Brown told them simply and straightforwardly and repeated several times the medical details.

He said that there had been some doubt about the diagnosis which was the reason for the slight delay in telling them. Mrs Stephens sat with fists clenched. Though both parents were visibly shaken, they were initially extremely calm. They asked a few questions but it was obvious that they wanted to be alone and when I suggested that they had some time together and that we saw them later they gratefully accepted. The tears were coming and Mrs Stephens said that her mother was on the ward and she did not think she could tell her. I offered to go and see her.

While Mr and Mrs Stephens had time alone I went to see the grandmother in one of the side-wards downstairs. I repeated the main facts as Dr Brown had given them to her daughter. She was stunned, and took hold of my hand as I told her. She and her daughter are very close; her own second baby — a son — had died soon after birth and she could not have any more children, so there had been tremendous rejoicing when a baby grandson had been born. She asked a few questions and then said that she would like to sit in silence for a while. I offered to make her a cup of tea, which she accepted. As I returned with the tea her son-in-law came in and said that her daughter would like her to go up. She sipped some of her tea because she was shaking and then she took my arm and I walked up with her.

Later Dr Brown, the houseman and I were asked to go back and speak with them all again. Mrs Stephens had cried a lot but was more relaxed now. They both asked many questions about the condition and how it would affect their baby and their own future life. After the doctors left I stayed and we discussed feelings and reactions. Both acknowledged that they felt numb and we talked about the phases of disbelief, depression and anger which accompanied crisis. Mr Stephens said that he could not go back to sea because he was needed at home but I encouraged him to think about compassionate leave for the moment and then to look at the implications for the future when they had had time to think round the problem. Mrs Stephens had some milk to express but was fearful of going back to the ward and having to face the other mothers. She wanted to go home with her husband but also wished to breast feed Peter. We talked about this and I said that the other mothers would find her return difficult because by now they would realize that something was wrong and would not know what to say to her. Mrs Stephens went back to the ward while the other mothers were out feeding their babies and when they returned she was able to tell them. This was the first hurdle successfully over.

Day 4

I arrived at the same time as Mr Stephens, who had brought some freesias in for his wife. Both were feeling much better, but if anything were a little too euphoric. Mrs Stephens had been given sleeping tablets last night, and as she said, 'had gone out like a light'. Mr Stephens had gone home with his mother-in-law and they had had some brandy and then he had been able to ring close friends and relatives and give them the information. We talked over the queries of last night and established that Mrs Stephens was more resigned to staying in hospital until Peter had got his feeding routine established. They were more receptive to taking each day as it came for a while and not rushing into taking any firm decisions. I arranged to see them on Monday morning.

Day 6

Mr Stephens had been given compassionate leave, the length of which was to depend upon Dr Brown's recommendation. Mrs Stephens spoke about the stages she had gone through over the week-end, including disbelief, and we discussed the mourning process. She mentioned a friend who had had a miscarriage recently and who was so depressed that they had taken her to the doctor. We looked at the links between mourning the loss through abortion and her needing to mourn the loss of the normal baby which she first thought that she had, and that a reactive depression could be a common factor in these situations. She said that her husband was feeling very low yesterday but his parents had come down and she thought this had helped him to get things more in perspective. Sunday had also been the day that her own mother had been able to break down and really weep for the first time since knowing of Peter's condition.

I talked with her about how the professional helping services could be used to assist a family with a handicapped child to live a life as near to that which they had mapped out for themselves had they had a normal child. Mr Stephens loves life at sea and was planning to take his Master's ticket. They knew that he would not get such a well paid job ashore but Mr Stephens did think that Peter would need his ongoing rather than his intermittent care. We looked at the fact that most children needed to have a father around and how this could be a problem for the families of sea-going fathers, but there had to be a balance between children's needs and father's careers and somewhere also some consideration of mother's happiness. I said again that I thought they should continue to live from day to day for a while and then begin to look forward and see if their plans had to be modified to fit in with the new situation created by having a child with Down's syndrome.

## Day 7

The results from Bristol were positive. Dr Brown and I saw the parents together for nearly an hour. There could be no more doubts and no more flights into the world of 'it may not be true', and from that time we were able to really look at the true implications of it all. Perhaps, more important was the fact that they were well prepared to do this and it was a most constructive interview. Mrs Stephens was to be discharged later that day but Peter had to stay in for a while until his weight increased and his feeding was established.

## Week 2

Mr and Mrs Stephens came in regularly, and did much for Peter. When he was ready to go home his mother came into the flat for 24 hours to take over his complete care.

## Month later

I visited the family at home. All was going very well and the grandparents were staying. Mr Stephens compassionate leave seems to be never ending, but now it is because a ship is not available. It has really given this couple the opportunity of making an excellent start with the daily management of their son. They had asked for something to read about Down's syndrome so I took them a copy of 'Bernard' by John and Eileen Wilkes. I told them that I thought it was an honest, well written account of their experience of bringing up a son with Down's syndrome but I did not know when parents should read it and would be glad to have their comments on this in due course.

We talked about the future social work contact. They understood that I had been actively involved at the beginning to help them adjust to the birth of a handicapped child. They knew I was the social worker for handicapped children and that I would see them when they came up to the hospital for the out-patient appointments. We were agreed that for the first year at least the problems with Peter would not be all that different from those of the normal child and likely to be for the Health Visitor, but that when he got towards his third year and educational assessment began there may be more social work to be done.

The third case was notable initially for the father's personal difficulty in coming to terms with the diagnosis and then for the change in the method of working necessitated when the baby's situation altered dramatically. The mother was a State Enrolled Nurse and had realised that there were some odd characteristics in her baby and had asked Sister who had been forced to give her some information, and had arranged for both parents to be on the ward when Dr Fergus did his round that morning. He examined the baby in the nursery and confirmed the diagnosis. Sister told him that the mother had a fear of mongols having once been chased by one, and had never been able to touch one in her nursing career.

## PARKER FAMILY

### Day 1

Both parents were in the ward and we had to speak with them there because the mother had a drip up. Mrs Parker had been crying. Dr Fergus said that it was as she had suspected and the baby had what is known as Down's syndrome. Mr Parker immediately asked why and whose fault was it, so Dr Fergus drew a chromosome pattern for him and explained about the additional one to the normal forty-six and how this was attached to the one known as trisomy 21. We spent a long time trying to establish that it was a freak of nature and nobody's fault and that it was not justifiable to do an amniocentesis test on every pregnant woman. Mr Parker asked what the future risk would be, although adding immediately the comment that there would not be any more children, not after this. He felt that he could not face the stigma of having to admit to his daughter being a mongol, nor did he think at the moment that he would be able to tell his own family. Both parents spoke about their two-year-old son being so bright and so forward.

Mrs Parker had met another mother of a mongol child when she had been going to the local infant welfare clinic and had been told that they found the facilities in this area so bad that they were moving to Birmingham where they believed services were much better. Dr Fergus and I both denied that the local facilities were inferior to those elsewhere and we thought that the special schooling in particular was very satisfactory. Although we spoke a little about the future, we urged them to be concerned with the here and now and to leave future planning for the time being. They asked what was the life span of a mongol and seemed surprised that she would reach adult life.

I stayed and spoke with them about the information that they had received. Mr Parker was shaken, very angry and very rejecting. Mrs Parker was the stronger personality of the two, and although she had wept and been distressed in the discussion with the consultant, she was much more realistic about what had now to be faced. We talked about what life for them could be like and why special schooling was necessary. Mr Parker asked if she would ever marry and when told that this was unlikely he seemed to find this extremely hard to face. I asked him if he had seen the baby and he said that he had not and did not want to 'after what had hit him when he came in.' When I pressed him gently to explain this he said it was seeing a Roman Catholic Irish padre coming out of the ward and then his wife saying that she did not think the baby was all right. (The significance of this apparent antagonism to Roman Catholicism and the Irish did not register with me until much later when I knew that Mrs Parker was a strong Catholic and had many relatives in Ireland.) I suggested that he came to the nursery or we asked Sister if she would let the baby come into the ward. Mr Parker kept referring to the baby as 'it' so I asked if they had decided on any names. Mrs Parker said Fiona Mary and then turned to her husband and said, 'It is still going to be that?' He nodded.

Sister wrapped Fiona up in a shawl and brought her in. Mrs Parker took her and her husband looked closely at the baby and then commented that one would not know. I agreed and added that it was only his wife's nursing experience that had made her aware. He looked at the eyes and ears, fingers and toes but would not touch her or hold her. Mrs Parker rocked her and cuddled her and talked about pretty pink dresses with ribbons and how they would make her into a beautiful baby. Mr Parker then asked if babies like these could be placed for adoption and his wife immediately responded by saying, 'You're not thinking of doing away with her are you, Roger?' He shook his head but he asked me again and I talked about alternative care and he seemed reassured that we were not saying that he had got to accept this baby and look after her and love her because she was his. We were understanding that part of him was feeling very rejecting of this baby and that he needed time. His ambivalence became apparent when he swung to the other extreme and commented that he supposed there was a danger that he would love her too much because she was as she was and the other child could miss out.

## Day 2

Mr Parker had to go to London on business, which was perhaps the best thing that he could have done at that stage. Mrs Parker had just finished breast feeding Fiona when I went in and was sitting cuddling her. She was feeling much better and spoke of mongolism being a challenge but she realized that it was going to be much more difficult for her husband. The hurt she had felt the day before when he had asked about adoption was mentioned again and I said that he would need time and may never fully accept the situation. Indeed there may be a part of both of them that would continue to grieve for what might have been. Mrs Parker spoke of her mother dying of cancer at the age of forty-eight and that it had been her role to hold the family together through this and she had learned to be strong. Personal suffering was not something new to her.

## Day 3

Fiona is looking jaundiced and the breast feeding is not going well but today her father came in and held her so progress is being made on this front. When I spoke to Mrs Parker later she referred to the reading she had done previously on handicapped children and decided that as they all had such horrors of the word mongol she would in future speak of the condition by the proper name of Down's syndrome. I gave her a cutting from the previous evening's local paper which showed the May Queen crowning ceremony at the local special school. The little girl who was being crowned was a Down's syndrome, albeit a high grade one, and Mrs Parker was delighted that it all looked so normal, although I explained to her that that little girl's intelligence was perhaps above average for children with that condition. It seemed appropriate to be concentrating on the more optimistic aspects of the situation at this point.

## Day 6

I saw Mrs Parker briefly before she went home. The breast feeing had not established and she had been disappointed that she had had to stop. They are planning to sell their house and move into the city so that they can be near good schools for both the children. I arranged to visit them at home in a month's time.

## Month later

Fiona was lying sleeping on her father's knee and looking very petite and pretty. Her features are not yet very pronounced and she is an attractive baby. Her brother was supposed to be in bed but when he heard me arrive he came down and sat on my knee for a while.

Mrs Parker is still much more realistic about Fiona's condition. Mr Parker believes in miracles (but not a God) and thinks that with the use of science these problems can be mastered. He spoke a little wildly about private education, keeping Fiona at home and employing private tutors who would help her to develop her potential. He was sure that if there was continued stimulation an above average intelligence could be achieved. Their house is sold and he is looking for a larger one with land so that they can keep ponies and other pets for Fiona. He nurtures a belief that with a lot of freedom and individual care she will be normal. We talked about the provision made by the state for the mentally handicapped and that the private sector was less likely to meet their needs, but he remained convinced that if one is prepared to pay, the best can be obtained and the best will make his daughter at least equal. He asked if she would have babies and that if she was 'a cracker with smashing legs' would he have to watch her with the boys. He did not really want to know that these children were sub-fertile but sometimes it was necessary to consider putting them on the birth-control pills.

It was in this interview that the stress in their marriage became very obvious. Mrs Parker is a devout Roman Catholic and her husband an atheist, although amenable to his children being baptized into the Roman Catholic faith. She is keen to have another baby and he is against this, saying that no matter what the odds were against this happening again the risk is too high. He argues that if there were another baby all the time that Fiona's needs would not be met. A part of him lives in a fantasy world and his essentially pragmatic wife finds this difficult to cope with; this leads to disagreements. It would appear that the arrival of a handicapped child had been an additional stress.

3 months later

Fiona came for her routine out-patient appointment and I saw her family in clinic as arranged. Mr Parker was too busy at work to come but his parents brought the family up. Dr Fergus was on leave and his registrar was taking the clinic. Dr Martin had done a higher degree in chromosomal abnormalities and he has a skill in being able to explain the most complex things in a simple meaningful way, and this he did with Mrs Parker. After examining Fiona he told Mrs Parker to bring her back to clinic in a month's time. While Fiona was being dressed outside he told me that the heart murmur was pronounced, the liver enlarged and the baby was in heart failure. When asked he said that he had not told the mother because Fiona was Dr Fergus' patient and he did not know how much information the parents had. I had been with them when Dr Fergus had spoken to the parents and although he had mentioned that the baby had a slight heart murmur and this was a common feature of Down's syndrome, they had not been told anything that would be as alarming to them as this information. We agreed that if when I went out to Mrs Parker, she seemed concerned he would speak with her again.

Mrs Parker's first words to me when I appeared were, 'Why does he want us back in a month; is there something wrong?' I suggested that if she was feeling anxious she should have another word with the registrar and I went to get him. He came out to a quiet part of the waiting area. Mrs Parker looked him straight in the eyes and said, 'Why?' and he looked her equally straight in the eyes and answered, 'Why indeed?' then they both smiled and sat down to talk. He explained that the heart murmur was pronounced today and that he thought Dr Fergus ought to examine Fiona soon and talk with them about this. He did not mention heart failure or poor prognosis but without causing undue alarm laid open the way for any further information that might have to be given to this family.

It also initiated a change in social work intervention. Up to that afternoon the focus of the work had been to help the family integrate a handicapped member into its future life. Now it would need to move towards initiating an anticipatory mourning process since it was almost certain that Fiona would not live to her first birthday.

Two episodes of hospitalization for chest infection and heart failure were soon to follow. During the second Fiona was seriously ill and had two attacks of apnoea. The houseman told the parents that if she stopped breathing again there was a very real danger that they would not be able to get her going again, whereupon Mr Parker asked what they should do if this happened at home. If he was hearing the ominous news he was not letting it be meaningful to him. He tended not to come into hospital and Mrs Parker was very torn between trying to meet his needs at home and those of Fiona in the ward. At times she felt unsupported without any of her own family near and her husband always being so busy in the business. She acknowledged that Fiona was hardly thriving, having only gained 5 ozs. in three months and that the situation could go either way. When both parents were seen together the stress between them was overt and they both admitted to being 'under the weather' and to having awful rows with each other. They spoke of the tension created by always listening for the 'phone to ring. Sometimes Mr Parker's thought processes seemed quite illogical and he still had no real understanding of Down's syndrome, nor of the heart condition. He made remarks like 'If she lives to be a year she will go on living.' He frequently complained of not being told anything. All this Mrs Parker found very difficult to deal with and kept telling her husband that he knew as much as she did, and she thought that was as much as anyone.

One of the cardiac consultants from the Brompton Hospital was coming to do his routine out-patient clinic and it was arranged that he would come up to the ward afterwards to study the various test results and to examine Fiona. After discussing the findings both consultants and I went to see the parents. They were told that Fiona had considerable pulmonary hypertension and a large ventricular septal defect, and that the prognosis was very poor. Mr Parker asked if there was a time limit and was told weeks rather than months. After the consultants left I stayed with Mr and Mrs Parker. He was dazed and she cried a lot. Several times she asked her husband if he was all right but he did not seem able to give his wife any comfort or support. At one stage as she wept and held Fiona close to her I put my arm round her shoulder and momentarily she leaned against me. Then she straightened up again. Mr Parker took Fiona and his knee briefly and then instead of giving her back to her mother he put her in her cot. We talked about how living with death would affect their lives. 'It will change everything', said Mrs Parker. They were due to move house in two weeks, and although Dr Fergus had said that Fiona could go home Mr Parker thought she ought to stay in hospital until they were settled. His wife disagreed and said that she would like to have her home and care for her herself. He argued that she would get the best medical attention in hospital. His wife did not deny this, but said that Fiona would get more love at home.

Two days later Fiona went home. I had a long interview with Mrs Parker and we looked at the social work involvement and how the task had changed. Originally I had been trying to help her mourn the loss of the normal baby and now it was concerned with mourning the anticipated death. It was then that Mrs Parker told me that as well as losing her mother her fiancé had died, so Fiona's death would be the third time that she had had to face the loss of somebody whom she loved very much. In comparison she thought that her husband had had a relatively easy ride in life; until Fiona had been born nothing had happened to him which had caused any distress.

Her faith is a strength in the situation and we were able to explore a little our understanding of pain and suffering and that it was not necessarily always a negative thing. She believes that after suffering people can emerge with stronger and better personalities. Of the two she knows that at the moment she is stronger than her husband but that he can be strong in some things and this is helpful to her. Her wish to have another baby was mentioned and despite her religious views she would agree to amniocentesis and, if necessary, abortion, for her husband's sake. She did not think that he should be exposed to this kind of traumatic experience again if it could be avoided.

There have been many tears in the last forty-eight hours, but at the same time Mrs Parker has emerged as a tower of strength to this family. Her friends and her sisters are rallying round and she is glad that they are moving so that she will not have to face well-meaning neighbours' enquiries about her little girl's progress. For Mr Parker his child's death might be easier to cope with than her long term handicap. In the five months of Fiona's life he never really got anywhere near understanding the implications of Down's syndrome but when the prognosis changed dramatically and he was told that Fiona would not live, he seemed to comprehend what this meant and respond appropriately. He became much more amenable to his wife's wishes and readily changed his mind about Fiona staying in hospital, and was able to support his wife in the decision that Fiona should spend the rest of her short life at home with with them.

## ROBERTS FAMILY

The fourth family had an older daughter who was seven. Their second daughter was early recognized as having Down's syndrome, and the parents were told by Dr Jones and me during the first evening. We planned the interview, and apart from making the mistake of not sitting the parents close enough together so that they could touch each other as they needed to, it went quite well. They were predictably shattered to begin with, used a long interview well next morning, and by the time that the mother was discharged after forty-eight hours much progress had been made. I did a home visit during the first fortnight and we arranged for the Health Visitor for handicapped children to join us for the first out-patient appointment. During this session we established with the parents what our respective roles would be and agreed that if all went along as expected for the first two years, I should maintain contact through the hospital appointments and the Health Visitor would visit at home and that we should all liaise. This pattern continued for the first six months and easily transferred to the new Health Visitor. At six months there was a short panic when Sarah had what was suspected as being an epileptic fit, but it was an isolated event. Sarah thrived and reached her milestones at a fairly normal rate. She smiled at two months, was sitting at nine months and soon after began to say Dada. Her sister would comment upon how Chinese she looked, and certainly it was apparent that she had Down's syndrome, but looks apart her first months were not all that different to what would have been expected with any baby. Sarah was a much adored little girl. Then disaster fell.

Two weeks before Sarah's first birthday

Dr Martin, the paediatric registrar, rang me at home at 11:15 p.m. to tell me that Mr Roberts had just brought Sarah into the ward and that she was dead. Mrs Roberts had had her first evening out in months and he had gone to look at Sarah last thing and had found her lying in an odd position after having obviously kicked off her bedclothes. When he went to straighten her he found her to be limp so he telephoned the ward and was told to bring her straight in. He had now gone home to collect his wife and to bring her back to the hospital.

I joined them and Dr Martin just after midnight. When I walked into the room Mrs Roberts' eyes filled with tears and she said, 'don't say anything'. I put my arm round her shoulder and said that I would not. She wanted to gain control again and when she felt that she had she was able to talk. There were a lot of guilt feelings around because the phenobarbitone tablets which Sarah had been having since her fit had run out the previous Friday and they had not picked up a repeat prescription until that evening. Dr Martin said that it was unlikely that this had contributed to the death, although it was possible that Sarah had had a fit. He spelled out what needed to be done. He would report the death to the Coroner and somebody from the Coroner's office would call round and see them in the morning. A post-mortem would be carried out and the Coroner would decide whether or not there had to be an Inquest.

Mrs Roberts asked if Sarah would stay on the ward and we told her that she would be moved, but did not say to where. I asked them if they would like to see Sarah again and they said that they would. There was a screen round the cot and they went behind it to make their farewells in private. When they came out Mrs Roberts asked if I would be seeing them again and I said that I would. I promised to telephone after the Coroner had been round. They shook Dr Martin's hand and thanked him. Night Sister gave them a polythene bag with Sarah's clothes in it which obviously caused them considerable distress. I walked to the door with them and checked that Mr Roberts felt able to drive home.

## Next day

I spoke first with Mr Roberts on the 'phone. He never says very much and did not today, but said that his wife would like to see me. I spoke with her and we arranged that I should go round at 7:30 p.m. when her daughter would be going to bed. However, when I did arrive the entire family had descended upon them unexpectedly and I was taken by the side door into the kitchen. I said that I was sure it would be more convenient if I called at another time but Mrs Roberts said that she wanted to talk to me then. Earlier I had spoken with the consultant and the main finding of the post-mortem was a small ventricular septal defect and this may mean that an inquest would not be asked for. He promised that he would telephone and arrange to see them and, in fact he did so while I was there. We talked about the post-mortem findings and Mrs Roberts latched on to the hole in the heart as being the cause, rather than being a possible contributory factor. At this stage I thought that it was better to let this go and not provide any other interpretations. She had 'cried bucketfuls all day' which was good and she cried during the interview. It had not been their year; first

Sarah had been born handicapped then her younger brother had had a carcinoma diagnosed and been operated upon and given radiotherapy. Her grandfather was dying of cancer in Scotland and her uncle had just gone into hospital for major surgery. Now Sarah had died. They were wondering if they were such wicked people that they were being punished for their sins.

We talked about the previous evening and she went through all the events of the day which had preceded the terrible trauma at the end of it. She spoke of the tremendous support she felt that she had had from Dr Martin and me, mostly because she knew us from previous moments of crisis, but also because we had had time to sit with them in the night when they felt that they needed us. She asked if Dr Martin was a family man and when I said that he was not married she half smiled and said that she could marry him. It was the first sign that some of the lost sparkle was to return.

Mrs Roberts told me that Sarah looked more of an angel in death than she had ever done in life. It had meant so much to her to see her again before they left the hospital but she had wanted to pick Sarah up and had not thought that she would be allowed. However she had kissed and cuddled her in the cot but something was not right and then she realised that it was the coldness of the body and she had wanted to pick her up and cuddle her close to herself to warm her up again. That day she had arranged with the undertaker that she would go and see Sarah before she was buried. She talked about her fears of mutilation in the post-mortem examination so I explained about the care that was taken and the repair work that was done afterwards. When I was asked if I thought her morbid I replied that it was important that she did what she felt was right for her. Some mothers wished to handle their dead child and the good thing about this was that they had a much clearer memory and knowledge that death had really happened. But in death bodies changed; they became cold, stiff and the colour altered and for some mothers this was a sight that they did not wish to see. Tears flowed as she spoke of not having got round to having Sarah christened and she wondered where she would be now. I told her what I believed and said that after death I could not accept that God differentiated between the baptised and the unbaptised. She had told her daughter that Sarah was with Jesus and she thought she herself believed this too. The funeral was not to be until the following week.

I said that I would make contact in a day or two and find out if she would like another talk. She said that it was so much easier to talk to somebody outside the family who did not steer her away from 'the things she wanted to talk about but which made her cry.' Again she spoke how how she had felt when I had walked into the room the night before she had been so glad to see me and yet at the same time she had felt all her grief welling up and this was why she had told me not to say anything. When I had put my arm round her shoulder she knew that I understood. Both grandmothers came in during the interview and had a chat. The elder daughter said hello but did not stay. I did not see Mr Roberts but was told that he was strong and coping all right.

Two days later

Dr Jones and I went together to the home to talk about the post mortem report. Although Sarah had had some heart defect he did not think that this was the cause of her death and that it must be regarded as a cot death and why this happens to babies is not known. For some reason they just stop living and for parents this is very hard. Mrs Roberts asked a few questions but her husband did not say anything, although he listened very carefully to what was said. Although he stressed that it was early days for thinking this way Dr Jones did say that they might in the future consider that Sarah's death was a blessing in disguise. Mrs Roberts said that she understood what he meant, but although she had been told it would be more difficult as Sarah got older she had not found having a child with Down's syndrome much of a problem so far.

I left with Dr Jones but I telephoned next day and we had a long talk about the cot death. Mrs Roberts said she found this so much harder to accept and, in fact thought that she had 'gone back a few steps'. I telephoned again after the funeral was over and we talked further about this, but by this time she was feeling less strongly that if she had been at home it would never have happened. She described the funeral and how she had dressed Sarah in her best clothes for it, although the undertaker had been very concerned that she might upset herself if she touched the body. Although her husband had driven her down he could not go into the room with her and had sat outside and waited. Her little girl had been 'playing up' and not going to bed and saying that she wanted to die and be with her sister. I explained that this 'acting out' was the little girl's way of mourning and that it was normal. They should try not to say that she was being silly but let

her talk about the things that were troubling her, particularly her
death fears which she was associating with going to bed. The days
are long for Mrs Roberts but the nights are worse and she is not able
to sleep. She thought that she might get a little job so that they could
save up for a headstone for the grave. I asked about coming to see her
and she suggested that we left it until after Christmas but said that
she would ring before then if she needed to talk.

Two weeks later — 'after Christmas'

I telephoned and arranged a time to visit. Mrs Roberts had a cup of
tea waiting for me, the house was immaculate as ever but Mrs Roberts
herself looked pale and heavy-eyed. During the day she tries to block
out any sad thoughts but when she goes to bed at night they all come
crowding back and she cannot sleep. She dreads going to bed so pro-
crastinates by having another cup of tea, reading a few more pages of
her book, listening to another record, watching more television or just
doing anything to postpone getting into bed and lying in the dark
thinking. For a while she was very sharp with her husband and lost
interest in him and nearly everything else, but this has improved. Part
of Mr and Mrs Roberts way of coping has been to put a taboo on the
subject and Mr Roberts will not talk about it with his wife because he
says it only upset her. But as she pointed out that does not stop her
thinking about it and she wants to keep on saying the same old thing
over and over again. We explored how she could use me in this process
and established that I did not mind how many times I heard 'the
same old thing' and in fact I thought there would be a slight change in
the way the same old things were said as time went along.

There are still tremendous problems for her in understanding why it
had to be a cot death and that it was not the heart which she had at
first been led to believe. We talked about being honest with parents
and whether or not they should be shielded from the really painful
information and she was quick to acknowledge that she needed to have
the whole truth. One of the most comforting things that she remembered me saying in that interview when she had been told of the cot
death was that although Sarah had died it would not be the end of our
contact with them. When I picked her up on this and said that she had
never telephoned me when she felt really down she smiled and said it
was knowing that I was there that was helpful. During the last fortnight
there had been times when she would have been glad to have had some

contact, but it had been Christmas, she knew I had a family and she knew I was going to ring her soon afterwards. We then established that there was a need for ongoing social work and that we should meet every two weeks primarily to talk through Sarah's death and her feelings about it. Meantime she agreed that if she continued to have difficulty in sleeping she would contact her General Practitioner for some sleeping tablets to help her back into a sleeping routine. When she felt better she would look for a part time job. At the moment she did not think she could face having any more children, not because she feared the pregnancy but because she dreaded the first year of the baby's life and the continuing anxiety about whether or not the baby is breathing. Everyone else seemed to think that she should have another child soon.

When a child is nearly a year old the loss is so much greater than it is with a newly born baby and the grief reaction is that much stronger. Close professional involvement with this couple at the initial crisis of being told that their newly born daughter was handicapped, and again when she came into hospital briefly following her convulsion, prepared the ground for the later work. When Sarah died suddenly we were quickly to hand and all the preliminaries of getting to know each other could be short circuited and the task of helping them to mourn could begin immediately. Mr and Mrs Roberts were familiar with social work practice, although it was Mrs Roberts who principally needed and was able to use it. She is intelligent and sensitive and most receptive to professional help. Her grief was great, and the fact that there was so much serious illness in the family at the same time probably accentuated the feelings she experienced when Sarah died. Her mourning will take longer because she lost so much more but at the end, with the help she uses so well, she should emerge as a strong person again.

*In your service of others you will feel, you will care, and you will be hurt, and you will have your heart broken. And it is doubtful if any of us can do anything at all until we have been very much hurt and until our hearts have been very much broken.*
MICHAEL RAMSEY, ARCHBISHOP OF CANTERBURY

The experiences in hospital and soon afterwards appear to be vital to parents' acceptance of the situation and their early treatment of the handicapped child. Furthermore they are likely to have bearing upon the parents' subsequent mental state, the child's own development and the parent-infant bonding process. As such their importance is immense and has warranted this close study of the process. The comments made by parents in the earlier survey provided us with guide lines and high-lighted possible pitfalls as we faced the difficult task of informing parents of an unfavourable diagnosis. But there could be no rules for doing this; guidelines, not tramlines, could be offered and there needed to be flexibility. Obviously this was a very limited sample, but the work recorded here demonstrates the value of very early team interventions in situations concerning loss, thereby enabling a family to mourn in a healthy way and to move towards an acceptance of the new situation.

Generally the planning of telling the parents was carefully followed and the team liaison was good. In the group where the babies died, although the original aim was to concentrate the social work intervention at the crisis point, there is evidence that in some situations it was terminated too soon. Where a mother was given an early discharge after only two or three days in hospital she ought to have been seen at home very soon afterwards. The follow up interviews, planned to occur a month afterwards and to be evaluating rather than therapeutic, sometimes indicated that the treatment had not been completed and as such were delayed too long. One couple (Harris) clearly needed more help at home earlier than they were given it, and only after two overdue interviews did Mrs Harris begin to move towards an acceptance of what had happened. There is no way of knowing if the professional help she received had any effect on the length of time it took her to mourn her loss, but perhaps better timing of it could have made her task less painful.

To some extent the seeming professional reluctance to extend the work into the home situation may have reflected another aspect of the survey findings. Those parents who had had social work help were asked to comment upon it. Several of them said that social workers did not seem to know why they were visiting, nor when to stop coming. Although I always said to this group of parents that they could write to us or telephone if we could help them in any way, with the exception of the father who made contact with the registrar about a previous pregnancy, none did so. It is more likely that the general debility they felt precluded them from actively seeking help, but if it had arrived on their doorstep it would have been acceptable. By contrast, in the second group where the handicapped child was expected to live the social worker was planning for on-going support, possibly for many years, and did not expose parents to the risks of too early termination.

Telling parents was seen as the beginning of a process that would lead on to the involvement of other professional workers, with the social worker acting as a key person in making the links.

Another thing that has emerged in writing up this work, particularly that with parents whose babies died was the frequent apparent neglect of the fathers' needs. Mothers are in hospital because they are the patients of the maternity department; fathers come as visitors, continue with their life outside and may not feel or be made to feel that they are so involved with the situation. It is believed that the bonding of fathers and offspring begins later and perhaps because of this the mother is the focus of attention in these early post-partum days. Although it was always the intention of the consultant and the social worker to see both parents together, and initially this was nearly always done, the subsequent work appears to have been done with the mothers and this may have reflected ease of access rather than need. In recording the interviews it is notable how often it was the mother who did the talking and how often the father sat in silence. The electroencephalogram result on one little baby showed that there was no brain activity controlling his body chemistry and that it was likely that he would die within a few days. His mother showed very little emotion about the situation, whereas the father was very upset whenever we spoke to them. The parents in this case were always seen together, yet retrospectively it is clear that the amount of work done was geared to mother's needs which were probably less than the father's needs. Similarly with the Green family, where Mr Green's stated dislike of the hospital situation meant that he did not come in very often. Yet after Keith died, though he was extremely upset, he was not seen again by the social worker, who focused on the mother in hospital. Mr Allen was much more upset than his wife in the first interview and when they were seen a month after the baby had died he was apparently still defending himself against the hurt caused by his loss. He was a naval father who said that they would deal with their grief, but it may have been that he would have been helped by more direct involvement on his own with the consultant. If service life encourages men to be men and not to display their emotions in public, then perhaps the caring professions should respond appropriately by providing the opportunity for a man-to-man talk.

Whenever the relatives came into the hospital at moments of crisis we involved them, with the parents' consent, in any discussion. We were always very aware of the fact that parents were part of an extended family, and that family usually would have an important role to play in supporting the couple in their grief. It was here particularly that the flexibility of the hospital routine was so good. Grandparents who were not usually admitted into the Special Care Baby Unit were allowed to visit their dying grandchild and to touch the baby if they so wished. Rooms were made available for relatives to sit together and there always seemed to be kindly ward ancillaries about who would make cups of tea at any time of the day or night.

One aspect of the work that parents did seem to find helpful was the explanation of what we were trying to do. Frequently the social worker explained the conceptualizations concerning mourning and what was the task of each of us in the process. It was not just somebody trying to be kind, but a person who knew something about the state that they were in and could predict how they felt and would feel as they worked through it. Likewise when there had to be a change in emphasis of intervention caused by a handicapped child who had been expected to live becoming a terminal case, this was shared with the parents. We would discuss how we had been working towards an adjustment in their family life to encompass the expected difficulties created by having a handicapped child, and recognized that this approach had to be changed to one of anticipatory mourning as they faced a premature death. It was frequently at this stage that parents ambivalent feelings overwhelmed them. Part of them felt saddened by loss, part of them was gladdened by being spared future problems, but most of all they felt terribly guilty about having had any feelings like this at all. It was very helpful to them to know that they were normal in this, that most parents felt the way that they did, that it was a usual reaction and that it would all resolve itself very soon. The apparent accuracy of prediction seemed to offer real security in the whole process of rehabilitation.

Teamwork and timing have been the two crucial factors. As we learned to work together as a team we recognized the skills and weaknesses of each other and of the team as a functioning unit. It was fortuitous for me that there was a group of consultants and registrars at the hospital in that year who were interested in trying new ways, and obviously the whole project depended very much upon their early anticipation and willingness to refer. We were not always in complete agreement as to the moment of telling, but were willing to be guided by the survey parents, who said sooner rather than later. We were agreed about honesty. Although we tried to give bad news as gently and as kindly as we knew how, we did not seek deliberately to shield parents by withholding the whole truth as we knew it to be. Honesty was crucial to the development of trust and this we believed to be essential with those cases where there would be ongoing involvement over many years.

It would probably have been impossible to support the parents in the early days in the way that we did unless we had been working as a team. Although we began as a group of people with clearly defined roles we were to become a unit in which members related well to one another and drew strength from the professional expertise of colleagues. At times we were very saddened by events but continued to be able to give real help to the parents because we had emotional support from a team membership. We discussed bereavement and loss and shared our feelings. It would be incorrect to say that we were not emotionally involved with some of these families, but we were never emotionally incapacitated. In our professional relationship with the parents we were sustained by the knowledge that any grief reaction we might experience would be delayed, any tears to shed would come later and that metaphorically there would be a shoulder to lean on.

If the professional people are sympathetic and helpful to the parents, the relationship formed during those first few days is very strong. It is important that the key persons who are going to give support and guidance over the years ahead are available during the time of initial contact. Professional bonding to the family may be equally as important a component of the rearing of a handicapped child as is the parental bonding. Many handicapped children are unable to show much response to their parents and the giving of emotion seems to be all one way. To sustain them in this one-way relationship parents need to draw upon relationships elsewhere. It may sometimes be appropriate that they are supported in this by the middle aged consultant and social worker who care for them in a professional way.

## POSTSCRIPT: THE PARENTS' PERSPECTIVE

A year later I wrote to all these families and asked if I might visit with a questionnaire to evaluate their experiences with the hospital team twelve months earlier. With the exception of one couple with whom we had had only relatively brief contact and who had subsequently moved to the Midlands, all agreed to do this. For those families whose child had survived I used the same questionnaire as had been used in the original handicap survey, and for those whose baby had died it was an adapted version focusing upon the loss through death aspects. Every interview was tape recorded.

The Coopers were a couple who had lost a premature baby two hours after delivery and were not referred to the social worker until just before Mrs Cooper was to be discharged. As they had moved house they had not received my letter asking if I might come but when I traced them through the help of a neighbour they were quite willing to answer the questions there and then. Mrs Cooper was feeding her baby son who had been born just a year after the other one died. She recalled being totally confused at the time of her son's death and had not been able to sort out if they were telling her that he would or had died. The worst part had been that she was put into a side ward on her own and had not seen any one all day except the cleaners who had said, 'never mind, love'. Mr Cooper had not known that in their circumstances he would have been allowed to stay with his wife. Mrs Cooper did remember a social worker coming but could not recall what was said. Her husband said that he could answer that because one of the first things that his wife had said when he had collected her was that somebody had been to see her who was very nice and had offered to come to see her at home if it would be helpful in any way. She had not needed this because she had a husband and her own family and she did not want to talk to anyone else. Occasionally they still get upset and they had been anxious about the last pregnancy until it had got beyond the thirty-week stage, which had been when they had lost the other one, but in all other respects they felt well and fully adjusted to what had happened.

The other family with which very little social work had been achieved had also had a premature infant, but this one had lived for much longer and the stress of this baby's battle for life had aggravated an already strained marital relationship. Mr Old was away on business at the time of the interview. Mrs Old could not remember the names of any of the people who had spoken to her and did not think that she had ever been told that the baby would not live. In fact, she felt that she had been given too much hope of there being a chance that the baby would survive. From the first moment that she had seen her, Mrs Old said, she knew the baby did not stand a chance. Her husband had had more contact with the Special Care Baby Unit because, post-operatively she was not allowed to move very far and when she got home she felt very depressed and low. Mr Old had been angered by the delay he had experienced in being given any news of his wife and child, and later they had both felt aggrieved that their other children and the grandparents had not been allowed into the nursery. Mrs Old had not found it helpful to have any contact with a social worker because she ·liked to keep things to herself, but she thought it helped her husband a great deal to have somebody to whom he could talk. They never mention the baby to each other now, and had not done so on the anniversary of her birth or death. Mr Old had had a vasectomy so there would never be any more pregnancies; their marriage was pulled right apart and she felt older, harder and lacking in a sense of humour.

It was interesting that Mrs Old should agree to do this interview after her not very happy contact with the hospital in the past. She said that she very much regretted not having a picture of her baby so I promised to ask the consultant if she could have one from the medical records. We sorted out the one that to us seemed the least traumatic and a few days later I took it round. I think it may have gone a little way towards healing the breach she felt between herself and the hospital.

## Allen Family

Although Mr and Mrs Allen had moved away from the area for nearly a year they had just been posted back. Their second baby was due in a month's time and the amniocentesis testing had revealed no abnormalities in this one.

They could not recall ever having been told that their baby was going to die, or 'be left to starve to death' as Mr Allen put it with some feeling. 'Nobody actually said that this baby will die or we are not going to do anything and because of this it is going to die. Therefore you might take the view that it might be a week, a month, two months or whatever — . If only someone had said we don't know how long it will take but she will die. I was terrified of being left with a baby who was still alive a year or two later — when they said that it had a massive spina bifida which was too large to operate on we got the hint quite soon that it was not going to survive.' Mrs Allen continued with this theme; 'Nobody told us when she arrived that it wasn't quite right. It was a breach and they said that as a breach usually has to be resuscitated Peter was sent out of the delivery room. I never cottoned on, but you know how you have your legs up for the birth and they put a cloth up so that I couldn't see it being born and immediately it was born they took the baby next door. They were all chattering away and everything and I said, "What have I got?" and nobody said anything to me. Then they said, "Oh we've just taken it next door to have a look at it." It was ages and I was asking questions and asking questions and saying, "Is the baby all right?" and he kept on sewing me up and when he had finished stitching me I said again, "Is the baby all right?" and the nurse said, "Well, baby is not quite right; your husband will be in to see you in a minute."'

Mr Allen took up the saga from there; 'There was no set up to tell me immediately. I was sitting in the corridor about half an hour after the delivery. Then a Sister walked straight out and passed me without looking and I thought there is something wrong; everyone was rushing around and I knew that something was wrong. In the end the bearded young paediatrician told me and asked who I would like to tell my wife and I said that I would like to. When I said to the doctor, "What sex is it?" he said that he did not know. That was worse. We thought, "My God, it is so deformed that you can't even tell that." I was expecting something far far worse.'

When they were asked if they had been told at the right time both parents said no and that it should have been earlier. 'It should have come out straight away; it's hell not knowing.' Although they had been given some information by the houseman, it was not until the following morning that they saw the consultant and the social worker. The first joint intervention is confirmed by the parents as being too late, as was suspected by the social worker. Both felt that they had had sufficient help from the hospital, and 'would have disliked it if we had been pestered every three minutes by busy bodies coming and saying, "Oh can I come and do anything for you." You don't want people to do that; you want to feel that you can handle it even if you can't. My personal reaction is to be left in a corner to do my own thing; I just regarded it as a medical problem being overcome.'

In their evaluation of the social work intervention there was perhaps a slightly differing reaction. Mrs Allen spoke about 'it's being nice to know that there was somebody there to cry on if we wanted to but it was not imposed upon us when we did not want it.' They felt that the service was adequate but there was nothing that a social worker could do because it was something with which they had to cope. When asked for their impression of what a social worker does, Mr Allen had some interesting comments to make:

'I think they are there to support those families which can't support themselves in a moral sense. A family should do the job instead of a social worker; basically the social worker is standing in for the old family unit as it used to be. Let's take us; we lose a baby. Let's assume we are a highly emotional pair, we're very sad and you come along and give us all the support that we need and we end up needing to have a little social worker and suddenly we find we like it, its nice, we can lean on our little social worker. Then we find that we are leaning on her for the next six months whereas if we had been left for the twelve hours we would have found that we had to get cracking and we'd never have needed her at all. There's the stigma too; social workers are for problem families — even if we had needed it I'd have been tempted to say scrub that. I don't like the idea of social workers; it's not my scene and I don't want to be involved.'

Mrs Allen had some minor gynaecological problems so had not conceived for six months. 'I was scared stiff I was not going to get pregnant again, especially when it took so long. We tried to plan it so that it didn't happen when he was at sea. We would not accept I was pregnant until we knew that we weren't going to lose it; there is much less rejoicing in the family this time, they are waiting and seeing.' Three weeks later I had a message from Mrs Allen to say that she was in hospital and would like to see me. She was delighted to show me her beautiful baby daughter and to tell me that the champagne was flowing on a certain ship in Her Majesty's fleet.

## Williams Family

Mr Williams had gone to see his mother at the time I had suggested seeing these parents and when I raised this with Mrs Williams she said that he had wanted to phone and put me off but she had persuaded him not to because she had wanted to answer the questions. He felt that it was 'a bit nosy parker' but she had thought it would help the hospital and was pleased to do it. Mrs Williams was expecting another baby in three months time. 'This one is all right; I've had the test done and I can feel the difference in the baby itself.'

She remembered that it was the young lady doctor who told them about their baby. 'I knew that something was wrong because I'd seen her feet. They didn't answer me when I asked them what was wrong with her feet. I'd liked to have been answered when I asked. Then she came right back in after they'd taken the baby out and I was glad about that and glad that they told me early. It was fairly blunt — "you've had a little girl but she's a spina bifida and she is expected to die." My husband went out after and he spoke to her. He asked if it would be definite that she would die and she said that it was because they would not be feeding her. He asked because he was glad that she was going to die: he didn't want her to live.'

Although Mrs Williams said she had sufficient help from the hospital staff she did feel that pressure had been put upon her to go and see her baby. She remembered having only one contact with the social worker, and did not think her husband had ever seen one. 'It was not necessary for the social worker to talk to me because she did not know enough about the case,' but then added spontaneously that it had been helpful to talk. She added that a social worker 'would be good with the right person — somebody who needs somebody to talk to. I didn't need any help from the hospital; I just wanted my family around me.' In considering the long term effects of the baby's dying, Mrs Williams said, 'Because I never seen her it was a lot better for me. I would have grieved more had I seen her. It was like a bad dream. Then I felt sort of guilty because I had had a little girl, she was ours and because she was abnormal we didn't want to know. That wasn't how we were thinking but that was how I felt — she must think that we don't want to know and I felt awful about that. I'm still glad that I never — after she had lived five days I thought that she would live and then I didn't want her to die. Then you phoned us and said that it was all over. I hope you don't mind me saying this but there was one thing that was wrong and that was when you asked us to come and pick up the death certificate and you started talking about the autopsy and I'd have rather waited until we came in. My husband never cried; instead of getting upset he gets angry. He doesn't understand why I cried so much; he says that its an everyday sort of thing — he's very deep in what he thinks but he would not talk about it until I got pregnant again. He says "all right, all right forget it, just look forward to this one." He bought me a cat and he sits and nurses it ... Nobody went to the funeral but we sent some flowers; we couldn't just let her be buried, that was our bit.'

As I was leaving Mrs Williams took me into their bedroom and showed me a cupboard beautifully made by her husband for the baby's clothes, the cot which he had stripped down and renovated and then gone out and bought a new mattress. As well as being real craftmanship it was a gesture of love and caring from a man said never to cry and only to express his emotion by getting angry.

## Field Family

Mr and Mrs Field were expecting another baby in the next few months and although they would like to discuss their earlier sad experience they asked that the interview be postponed until after the new baby had arrived and they were sure that all was well this time.

## Green Family

After having lost three babies before, Mr and Mrs Green both said that their earlier experiences made them adjust to the loss of Keith very quickly. In fact Mrs Green thought that she was over it by the following morning. Her husband took slightly longer. 'I came home and next day I had to go and sort everything out. It was the second time that I had registered a child's death and at dinner time I broke down to her mother; by evening it finally struck home that we weren't going to have one home and the following day it was all right, except I started smoking over forty cigarettes a day.'

Their only major regret was that the previously agreed sterilization had been carried out. 'I wish the paediatrician had come down and explained the baby's chances when I was in early labour — if I had known his chances were poor I'd have had another. Apart from coming home from hospital without the baby's name band, Mrs Green was also sorry that she had not held him. 'When he was dead and we went to see him I'd have liked to have held him; holding his hand through the hole is not the same.' Mr Green did not remember having any contact with the social worker but his wife recalled having seen her every day and had appreciated 'the motherly view of whats happening rather than a clinical view.' She thought that things had been put into layman's terms and there had been liaison made with the doctors and nurses.

## Thompson Family

It had not been an easy year for the Thompson family. Mr Thompson had been involved in a road accident, and Mrs Thompson had had a brief spell in hospital for minor surgery. They were still living with his mother because they had not been able to get a place of their own.

Mrs Thompson had not returned to work.

They thought that the hospital team had been very helpful to them and could remember very clearly who had been involved and when they had seen various people. The contact with the social worker 'helped us a lot' but both felt that it had been about six months before they began to get back to normal again. Mr Thompson had begun to drink very heavily after Michael died and this had been the cause of his road accident. For both of them there was still considerable sadness about their decision that 1:4 risk is too high to contemplate further pregnancies. When this was discussed Mrs Thompson cried. They had talked about adoption, but did not think they would be good enough, and about fostering, but they did not think they could face this because when 'they went away it would be just like Michael dying.' For them the loss was not just one baby but the whole possibility of subsequent children and for a couple who had hoped to have two or three children this was a great sorrow. They thought that they were getting over Michael's death but at times they still got upset and felt that they would never make a complete recovery.

Harris Family

Mr and Mrs Harris were expecting another baby in four months time and both were 'a bit anxious about this one'. Despite their great grief at the time of their first baby's illness and death they had clear recollections of what had happened and with whom they had been involved. They remembered the houseman and me seeing them and that one of the most helpful things that had been done was to have their baby baptized. 'It was nice to think that she was christened and had a name and that we were there.' They had appreciated having an opportunity to talk with the social worker and at a later date with the health visitor. 'As soon as they come in they don't talk about little things, they get right down to the heart of the matter.' When asked if that was helpful they replied, 'Well it depends – it takes you by surprise; you've never had anything like it before. Nobody round here mentions it; the neighbours avoid saying anything and then the social worker says how about Tracy right out – but it *is* the only way.'

Mrs Harris still got upset when she thought about Tracy, and at times in the interview she cried. Her husband had suggested to her beforehand that if seeing me would bring it all back would it not be better to cancel the interview, but she had wanted to go ahead. After their annual holiday she had returned to work and this had helped her to feel much better; by Christmas when she knew that she was pregnant again she was beginning to feel somewhere near being back to normal. She admitted to being extremely anxious in this pregnancy and although she said that the actual delivery did not worry her at all, the thought that she might be separated from her husband and baby afterwards was creating much stress. Obviously some special concessions about visiting were going to be needed to get this couple through the next confinement and they agreed to being referred to the maternity medical social worker.

Thorpe Family

A baby daughter was born to Mrs Thorpe ten months after Richard died. Her blood pressure went up slightly at the end of the pregnancy and she was admitted to be induced. There was much rejoicing in the whole family when the long awaited little girl arrived.

When they looked back to the two days when Richard had been so critically ill they said that everyone had tried to be helpful but because they had felt numb they had not registered anything. They had found their contact with the social worker to have been helpful, 'nice just to talk to' and this the relatives had appreciated as well, but both emphasized that with a family around which was so close they did not feel that they needed help in the same way as those who were lacking relatives. Both felt quite well again. They had made themselves carry on with all the things that they had done before and now were beginning to enjoy them again. Before they lost Richard they had been close, but now they said, 'Having been through that together we'd do anything for each other now.'

Of the four babies born with Down's syndrome only two were fit and well at the end of the first year. Sarah Roberts had died very suddenly just two weeks before her first birthday. Fiona Parker, having had a serious heart condition diagnosed at five months which was given a poor prognosis, struggled on through frequent bouts of colds and bronchitis and gaining no weight to reach her first birthday, much to the amazement of everyone concerned. However, Peter Stephens and Paula Cann made excellent progress in their first year and both reached their respective milestones at only a slightly slower rate than the average normal child. In each family the parents were very involved and able to maximize the potential in their child. In neither family situation was the condition proving to be much of a problem so far.

## Roberts Family

After Sarah's very sudden death I had continued to work with Mrs Roberts at decreasing intervals for nearly six months until we both knew that she was strong again and able to carry on in a well state. For Mr Roberts it was not necessary but he welcomed my involvement with his wife.

Their contact with the hospital on the night that Sarah died was only briefly over two or three hours but they were able to make some interesting comments about their unique experience. It had been helpful to them to be seen by hospital staff whom they knew and liked. They had always found the registrar and social worker to be dedicated people and 'as easy to talk to as ordinary people' and had been so glad that it was these two who were around that night. They had appreciated talking about it, had been grateful when we suggested that they might like to go and see Sarah, and had been sorry that we had not told them that they might pick her up and hold her if they so wished. Mrs Roberts had felt particularly dismayed when she had been given the carrier bag containing Sarah's clothes as she had left the ward.

As far as the social work could be assessed, Mrs Roberts summed up her feelings when she said, 'I've spoken to her so much and I've had all the help I needed. It was there for the asking and when I needed her she came. I suppose you could say that I had a social worker for the year of the baby's life. She was there at the time of telling us that our baby would be handicapped, there at the death and she came afterwards. I needed to talk about things and the social worker was ready to listen and it was helpful to me to do that.' Mr Roberts spoke about his personal attitude. 'I've always felt slightly detached — I'm a detached sort of person, sometimes more than at others. I'd answer the questions differently at different times. You've got to accept everything. Personally I've found it a very similar feeling to when I found out that Sarah was a mongol. That was just as big a shock to me as when she died. Perhaps I've withdrawn, even become a bit callous — I also believe it is better to be sorry about something immediately, then to phase it out, and to be practical. It happens to hundreds of people and you shouldn't dwell upon it. Compared with some of the disasters in the world it's a minor thing – this may be my cushioning, my mental cushioning, this could be how I get along because I think in this way. I feel sorry for her that she feels more sorry than I do.'

Although they do not talk about Sarah very much they share closely all other aspects of their life: 'We still enjoy a very happy relationship together.' For them the experience of having a handicapped child who lived for a year and then died drew them much closer together as man and wife. Mrs Roberts added, 'I'm still fearful for the future; will it happen again? But I am looking forward now instead of looking back and that includes moving into thinking about other children.'

### Parker Family

'I still think Fiona will make medical history in the end.' Mr Parker continued to believe in his miracle helped by the fact that on reaching her first birthday Fiona had defied the expert prediction of a leading heart specialist that her life span would be weeks rather than months. Her parents were looking back at two experiences of being given bad news. Clearly it was the second and in a way more devastating one which for them felt less traumatic. This was partly because the information, although confirming their worst fears, also ended the anxiety of not knowing, and partly because they were being told by people whom they now knew.

They had picked up early hints about Down's syndrome before the consultant told them. Mrs Parker had suspected it as soon as Fiona had been put in her arms and had asked the nurse if she was a mongol baby and had been told, 'Well you know I can't comment until the specialist has seen her.' That made Mrs Parker so suspicious that she asked them to telephone her husband and tell him to come in. Mr Parker continued, 'I'd got some flowers in my hand and the priest came out of the room and he looked at the flowers and he looked at me and he didn't say a word and I knew something was wrong. And then Sister said, "Fiona's a mongol," full stop, just straight out with it – it was an awful shock.' Then they saw the consultant and the social worker who had explained more about the condition to them. Both parents felt that they had been told at the right time generally, but for Mr Parker it had been the wrong moment.

Until Fiona was born Mr Parker thought that social work was something to do with social security and means testing and that a social worker was a nosey person who asked about money matters.

It was inevitable that he should be very confused when a social worker had come in with the consultant, and perhaps even more so by the fact that money matters were never mentioned. At first he had thought why is she here because it was nothing to do with anyone else other than the doctors and themselves. Then both parents had found that the social worker was the one person to whom they could talk and express their fears, and for Mrs Parker it was 'better than the immediate family. I couldn't have cried with his mother but I could with the social worker.'

It was not really until the second crisis that Mr Parker acknowledged that a social worker had been helpful to him. 'She made me stronger because she was there. I couldn't throw my arms round my wife which I knew I should have done because I'm not that sort of person. I'm not a lovey dovey sort of person but because she (the social worker) was there I felt a lot stronger in myself. It made me feel good and I knew that somebody's got to be strong in the family and it had to be me.'

Although Fiona's death always seemed to be just round the corner, both Mr and Mrs Parker were living a life as near normal as they could make it and enjoying each day as it came. There was nothing more that a social worker could do.

## Stephens Family

Having a handicapped child has altered our attitude — it's a complete turn about. Sometimes we wonder even now is this really happening? Two weeks after we were told we kept thinking — why? what's causing it? why me? The answers came a month to two months later.

Both Mr and Mrs Stephens freely admitted to needing help often and to being able to use relatives, friends and the professionals to try to meet this need. They acknowledged that much of their positive feeling towards the hospital team stemmed from their first contact, which they felt had been handled with sensitivity. They had appreciated being given some time together on their own after being told. 'I didn't cry until we were alone; it was partly pride, partly numbness, I didn't feel anything in a physical sense just numb. It was most peculiar. As soon as I cried it went but you still feel a little bit as if you're in an alcoholic stupor.'

Although we had suspected that fathers' needs might have been neglected, it was only Mr Stephens who actually mentioned this. 'After that evening whenever I went back to the hospital I felt a little bit left out. Everything in hospital is built around the mother and baby. The ward sister was absolutely super, allowing me virtually twenty-four hour visiting, but Dad does get left just a little bit in the cold. You're there on sufferance sometimes. Hospitals are kind but in a detached sort of way.'

Of the two key professional people in their case Mr and Mrs Stephens spoke with warm feelings. 'Dr Brown is not a typical consultant. He knows who you are and doesn't treat you as a file. He says hello to Peter in the waiting room and is obviously fond of him. He takes time and is so approachable. As for the social worker, I don't think we could have got through this year without a social worker and come through it as well as we have. It's a very useful non-medical backup, a good listener, somebody who knows what she is talking about without being medical. She sits and listens and doesn't try to answer everything. Friends are very good, they don't interfere but they do tend to keep coming back and saying, 'oh yes but — '.

## Cann Family

'The difficulties I can see in the future when she is a young woman but still a child. Perhaps we're in a false position because we've got no problems at the moment and we forget she is handicapped. At the moment we haven't got to face the problem because it doesn't exist. If you kept looking forward to the future problems you would never cope; if you just get on with how she is now it's all right.'

Once they had got over the bad introduction to the knowledge that Paula was handicapped, Mr and Mrs Cann got on with the task of bringing up their three children and found that in some respects their little daughter equalled the progress made by their boys in the first year. But they still look back to the way that they were told with considerable anguish. 'I was particularly concerned that Mary was told and I wasn't there. Paula was born soon after 8 a.m. and the midwife said she wasn't too sure about the baby and she was going to get the doctor to look at her and he'd be down in a minute to see us. When he didn't come we went to chase it up and find out what it was all about and ask if the doctor had seen her. The nurse said that the hands were a little bit blue but she was much better and they brought her in, but obviously the doctor had not seen her. I stayed in the hospital for most of the day and then I went home to take the choir practice. At a quarter to eight Dr Fergus came and told Mary that the baby was a Down's syndrome. Mary knew that there was no way of getting me because I was with the choir. I didn't get back till 9 p.m. and then she couldn't get the trolley phone so Sister let her use her 'phone in the office. She was on her own for over an hour, not able to get me and not able to discuss it with anyone. I couldn't see any reason when it had been left all day why it couldn't have been left until the following morning when I was with her. At that stage neither of us knew what it meant. I asked for information, but at 10 p.m. Dr Fergus was not available but his houseman came down. He was in a bit of a predicament because he thought Dr Fergus would want to tell us himself but he told us basically what Down's syndrome was in general terms. Obviously he couldn't tell us very much about our case. I think Mary ought to have had a night's sleep because neither of us slept that night.' Mrs Cann added that she thought they could have been told within an hour or two as soon as they suspected anything, but having left it for twelve hours leaving it a bit longer would not have made any difference. She said very firmly that, 'I still think the earlier the better.'

Perhaps partly because of their unfortunate initial contact with the consultant Mr and Mrs Cann have not found him to be very helpful to them in their first year. Although they had not seen the social worker very often they had found this contact made up for some of the seeming deficiencies in the medical one. Interestingly the consultant and the social worker usually saw the family jointly at the out-patient appointment, but the social worker always spent extra time either before or afterwards talking about any difficulties which may be arising. When asked their impression of what a social worker did, they replied that if they had been asked this question eighteen months before they would have said they were 'well off ladies with nothing to do other than going round dishing out alms to the poor and needy. But now we've met one and experienced the very specialized and professional work which goes on with the problems which can develop from illness, we have a very different impression. We've had advice, help, reassurance, moral support and perhaps most important we've had information. She was the only person who really gave us any information; the only person who told us what it would be like. It's been good.'

## REFERENCES

D'Arcy, E. (1968) Congenital Defects: Mothers' reactions to the First Information. *British Medical Journal* 3, 796.

Kew, S. (1975) Handicap and Family Crisis. Pitman London.

Kennel, J. and Klaus, M. (1970) Mothers Separated from their Newborn Infants. Pediatric Clinics of N. America 17, No. 4, 1015–35.

Kennel, J., Trause, M. A. and Klaus, M. (1975) Evidence for a sensitive period in the human mother. Parent – Infant Interaction (Amsterdam: CIBA Foundation Symposium 33, new series ASP).

McAndrew, I. (1976) Children with a handicap and their families. Child: care, health and development 2, 213–237.

Whiten, A. (1975) Postnatal separation and mother-infant interaction. (Paper presented at the conference of the International Society for the Study of Behavioural Development, University of Surrey).

Stokes, B. M. (1976) Helping parents to accept. *Child: care, health and development* 2, 29–33.

# Social Work with Children with Leukaemia and their Families

## PETER ELFER

### INTRODUCTION

During the long summer placement of my social work course, I worked on a paediatric ward in a general hospital. The first case I was given was that of a boy of eight who had just been diagnosed as having acute lymphoblastic leukaemia. In trying to offer help to this boy and his family many questions and dilemmas were raised regarding the nature of the help offered and how useful it was to the family. I decided to make this the subject of a study, in an attempt to resolve some of the questions and dilemmas raised by the first case.

As I did the preparatory work, it very soon became clear that the thinking behind the study would have to be guided by some direct feed-back from families that had actually cared for a child with leukaemia. The number of families coming for treatment to the hospital in which I worked was not large and of these only one or two could be approached for permission to interview them — one of course could not ask to talk to parents who had very recently lost a child or whose child was in a deteriorating state of health. I therefore approached paediatric social workers in two other hospitals to ask for help.

In all I had direct contact for three months with one child and his family during treatment, interviewed five sets of parents who had lost a child and six with a child who had been through treatment. I also spoke to three paediatric social workers: one was my supervisor and two were at other hospitals.

The objective of the study was to examine some of the issues involved in offering help to children with leukaemia and their families and

75

to compare the comments and feelings of parents with some of the written work in the field.

Two continuous themes emerged in the preparation of the study. I began with some very definite guidelines in mind for working with families with a terminally ill child – the child should be told honestly of the exact nature of his illness, and parents should be encouraged to speak openly of the illness in the family. These lost their priority in favour of two themes. One concerned the importance of gearing help not to external norms of what is 'psychologically healthy', but to the unique way a family copes with a crisis. Hollis, for example, might uphold principles of casework practice, but I have argued that a much more spontaneous flexible approach is essential. The second related but more general theme is that very few general rules or policies in the management of the family with a terminally ill child are possible. Perhaps the only one is the importance of offering help quickly – but situations that occur can be so threatening, painful or bizarre that responses have to be those that seem right and appropriate for the situation, however unorthodox.

I owe a great deal to the parents who agreed to let me, a complete stranger, enter their homes and question them about one of the most awful, painful episodes of their lives. Without the contribution they made, the study would have been almost worthless. The possibility of even asking these parents to meet me was made by the hospital social workers who helped me, by contacting parents on my behalf. The comments and ideas of parents being the body of the study, I regard my supervisor at the hospital where I was placed as the backbone. During the placement, he gave me a tremendous amount of support and understanding in working with families of sick children. After the end of the placement, I called on him many times for information, views and advice and on each occasion he spared a lot of time from a crowded day for patient discussion. I am glad of the opportunity to record (though necessarily anonymously) the extent of the help he gave me.

## THE FAMILIES

I visited eleven families in all. The interviews were very informal – I explained the work I was doing and why I was interested in children with leukaemia, and asked parents general questions about the way they had been told the diagnosis, what help they had received, what reactions brothers and sisters had shown and so on. Parents then mostly talked freely and fully without many further questions. I was normally ready to depart after an hour but all the interviews lasted at least two and, in one case, nearly four. I was concerned that the interview would be a painful burden to impose on parents, provoking memories and distress. Undoubtedly, the interviews were painful in some respects but several sets of parents said it had been helpful to tell a complete stranger all the events from beginning to end, with their associated feelings — I hope this was true also, to some extent, for the other parents.

* — Child with leukaemia

1. Mr and Mrs Anderson
   (Philip (16), Neil* (14), Clare (5);
2. Mr and Mrs Drew
   Richard (17), Gerald (14), Damien* (8);
3. Mr and Mrs Jacobs
   Ian (3½), Edward* (1½);
4. Mr and Mrs Kingston
   Mary (7), John (20 mths);
5. Mr and Mrs Long
   Patricia* (3), Terrence (14 mths);
6. Mrs Masters
   Michael* (10½), Jeremy (9), Jean (8), William (7);
7. Mrs Mathews
   Mark* (5), Susan (2);
8. Mr and Mrs Philips
   Sarah* (5);
9. Mr and Mrs Rodgers
   James* (8½), Simon (4½), Dean (2½);
10. Mr and Mrs Temple
    Michael (12), Steven* (9), Brian (6);
11. Mr and Mrs Thomas
    Christine (14), Linda* (11);
12. Mr and Mrs Wickens
    Matthew* (8½)

(All are pseudonyms)

## LEUKAEMIA: THE DISEASE

Leukaemia was first described and identified by a German pathologist in the mid-nineteenth century — the name meaning 'white blood'. The blood normally consists of a number of types of cells having different functions: red cells, carrying oxygen; platelets, inhibiting bleeding and white cells combating infection. The white cells are called leucocytes and have two varieties: lymphocytes and polymorphs. Leukaemia involves these white cells when they fail to divide or mature properly — lymphoblastic leukaemia when it is the lymphocyte variety affected, myeloblastic leukaemia when the polymorphs are affected.

The majority of all cells are produced in the bone marrow. When some are malforming, they have difficulty in passing into the blood and accumulate in the marrow. The accumulation prevents the production of the other cells — platelets and red cells. The total effect then is a lowering of resistance to infection, poor clotting properties so that bleeding is hard to prevent, and anaemia. Myeloblastic leukaemia is very much more severe than lymphoblastic. Leukaemia has an incidence rate of about 500 new cases in children per year.

Treatment is aimed at removing the malignant cells so that normal cell production and functioning can continue (if achieved, called a remission). One of the factors that makes leukaemia such a serious illness is the damaging side effects of drugs and the harm done to healthy cells by the treatment. The effects of treatment therefore have to be monitored very carefully, especially in the first months; this requires frequent blood tests, collection of bone marrow and cerebral spinal fluid, a liquid flowing in the spine and around the brain. This requires the insertion of a needle in the lumbar region penetrating to the centre of the spine to draw off liquid; the bone marrow collection requires the insertion of a needle, normally into the soft end of a bone. Both these procedures are very unpleasant and can often be painful.

An important advance in treatment in recent years has been radiotherapy. Drugs available were ineffective in killing cells in the cerebral spinal fluid, and the accumulation of leukaemic cells in the fluid led to meningeal leukaemia. This condition is very difficult to treat and greatly reduces life expectancy. Exposure to radiation daily for two to four weeks is very effective on the cerebral spinal fluid and has improved the prognosis. But this too is an unpleasant and frightening treatment: children, sometimes very young, must lie alone in a large chamber, surrounded by alarming machinery, and keep perfectly still. Side effects are loss of hair (which grows back) and sometimes drowsiness. Drugs also have side effects; fluctuation of appetite, soreness and mouth ulcers, skin rashes, cramps and pains and tingling, irritability and moodiness.

Overall, prognosis has improved tremendously over the last decade but it is difficult to say very much about current treatment regimes because little is known of what side effects may appear in children, say in ten years, or whether remissions will even hold for that length of time. However the possibility of a remission holding indefinitely seems good for about one in every two of the children in the best prognostic category, that is, in those children diagnosed between the ages of about three and ten, with acute lymphoblastic leukaemia, whose blood is in a relatively good condition at the time of diagnosis.

## TELLING THE PARENTS

The parent-child relationship in almost any family is such that when the child presents symptoms of illness some reaction of concern is caused. Mild illness in childhood is so common and one hears so rarely of fatal illness in children, that it is not surprising that parents remain fairly unalarmed when symptoms first present themselves. The parents I spoke to were all unconcerned when their children complained of aching joints, or had a slight rash or bad dose of influenza. Anxiety began to develop only when the symptoms remained after two or three weeks, when the general practitioner's treatment was ineffective and further investigation was needed. Consciously and sub-consciously it may be at this early stage that psychological 'worry work' first starts preparing parents for all that is to come. The increasing severity of the symptoms, the decision of the doctor to admit the child for further tests, the summons to the paediatrician all add to the increasing anxiety and speculation about possible diagnosis. So at the time of walking into the consultant's room, parents are very alarmed, and this is one of the main things to keep in mind when planning this first interview. Ross, in discussing counselling for the parent of an 'exceptional child', says, 'the interviewer will be walking into well prepared defences' such as denial, anger, and intellectualisation.[1] The interviewer is likely to be very anxious himself about the situation, and unless he has carefully prepared himself it will be very easy to show impatience or irritation to parents who seem emotionally untouched by the diagnosis or angrily deny it as nonsense.

To contrast two cases: James Rodgers developed symptoms rather slowly, and it was a matter of a few weeks before he was referred to a consultant and tests were completed. At the hospital Mrs Rodgers was asked to bring her husband, as the consultant wished to see them both. 'We knew then it was something pretty serious'. Mr Long, on the other hand, said it seemed as though Patricia went to bed well one evening and had deteriorated overnight. She was admitted to hospital very quickly but Mr Long refused to believe the diagnosis for several months. The lack of opportunity to prepare in any way is perhaps partly the cause of Mr Long's inability to accept the diagnosis.

Bearing in mind the comments of parents about their thoughts and reactions at the time of diagnosis, I have the impression of a kind of automatic protective screen slipping into place and isolating the mind from the subject of the interview: 'It was a young doctor and he did not really seem to know what to say' (Mrs Anderson). 'I remember thinking how well the doctor was doing his job — how well he was treating us and explaining things' (Mr Thomas).

Although it is difficult for the doctor and social worker to be available at the same time, I think it is valuable if they can appear together for at least a part of the first interview for a number of reasons. It increases the chances of the parents feeling a more solid commitment from the hospital to share in the care of their child; the social worker receives a first hand impression of the parents' reaction and is better placed to judge how to help afterwards and what details may need repeated explanation. There was some difference of opinion between the social workers I spoke to on the subject of joint interviews. One social worker thought that too great an alignment between the doctor and social worker might inhibit some parents from expressing anger or despair towards doctors, concerning medical care of the child. Another emphasized the importance of as much involvement as possible between parents, doctors and social workers towards the total care of the child and suggested such an approach was far more likely to enable the parent to express feelings than a separation of caring roles.

First questions after the doctor has seen the parents are fundamental ones. Why? How long has he to live? What treatment is there? What can we do? These are almost unanswerable in any digestible form because the answers are complicated and filled with 'ifs' and 'buts'. Answers need to be as short as possible. It is important to devote more concern to the parents who are upset and to emphasize preparedness to help with arrangements and to talk over problems that arise. It may be valuable to explain again some of the basic elements of treatment, if parents seem completely bewildered. Two parents had understood that there were seven possible combinations of drugs that could be tried and that, on average, their son had about three years to live, but at home they were quite uncertain whether this was three years for each combination of drugs in turn, giving him a life expectancy of twenty-one years, or whether just one combination could be used.

It is difficult to imagine the extent of shock, disbelief and confusion parents face – their form and depth are unique and in the first days, especially, have to be faced alone. What the social worker can do, if friends and relatives do not, is first ensure that the basic supplies for life – shelter, food, warmth and contact – are maintained and, secondly, to encourage parents to 'be upset' – not to struggle to control themselves or take false reassurance that everything will be all right.

The majority of parents expressed at least doubt about seeing a social worker at the time of diagnosis – some were astonished at the suggestion. 'What could they do? How could someone from outside the family who has not been through the same thing possibly know?' (Mr Philips). (Incidentally, at the end of our meeting Mr Philips said how helpful he had found it to talk things over and share their situation – he was surprised at his own change of attitude). 'We would have felt it an intrusion, I just wanted to be alone and later in the evening went out for a drive alone' (Mr Thomas). 'I do not think anyone could understand enough to be able to usefully help or listen' (Mr Anderson).

These are comments by parents who did not have any social work help. Those that did spoke very highly of the help they received. This was mainly because they knew they could be upset with the social worker, they did not have to be cheerful and they were given the opportunity to talk when they needed to – not when the social worker wanted them to. But they also wanted to be alone when first told the diagnosis. Despite this, it is still important to ask the parents: 'We did not want to talk but we wished someone had approached us and just asked if we wanted to discuss anything' (Mr & Mrs Long).

In the first days, then, all the social worker can hope to do is to be available at the time or very soon after the diagnosis is given, to be with the parents to introduce himself and talk over any immediate urgent problems or explain again any major misunderstandings; to ensure that parents have transport home, that they are able to visit, that they have family or friends at home to turn to, that they have basic supplies of money, food, and warmth. 'It was not until I got to the hospital door that I broke down and wept — I had borrowed 50p for the bus and went home alone crying' (Mrs Masters).

Two theoretical ideas on response to crisis

I would like to compare two statements concerning coping with crises as a useful way of thinking about intervention.

Margaret Robinson has written,

> Individually, each person has a characteristic set of responses and ways of dealing with stress. The richer the personality, the more variety there is within the repertoire, the poorer the more impoverished. Families, though more complex, seem to be the same. A turning point is reached when previously unrealised strengths are mobilised.[2]

Whilst the article from which this comes is concerned with the nature and importance of outside help at the time of the crisis, it seems that the author thinks coping skills brought to the crisis play a large part in its resolution. The results of research by Gerald Caplan lead to a different perspective:

> Whether a person emerges stronger or weaker is not necessarily determined by his 'character' or his inner strength but by the kind of help he gets during the trouble.[3]

These are two apparently different views of what is important in determining coping ability in a crisis. For the families I have spoken to, the views in practice overlap: the past experience of families in coping with crises and the value of the help they receive will influence how open and able they are to use help offered at the time of a new crisis. This is not to say that all the responsibility for receiving help rests with the parent — the helper must make help acceptable as well as available — but it is hard to receive help, and good past experience of being helped, of 'feeling feelings' rather than just talking of them, will obviously help parents to cope with despair and confusion that threaten to overwhelm them.

Although there is overlap, I think the two views are significant as individual statements. Associated with the importance of past experience of crises is the general background from which people come and the norms of family behaviour: roles at home, and their flexibility, the acceptability of expressing emotions, the quality of communication, and so on. When children are regarded strictly as the 'mother's department' (and of the parents I interviewed, role segregation and ways of coping did not correlate with any categories of class), it is more difficult to involve the father in treatment plans or counselling, than it is where a father is as concerned as the mother in the direct care of children. Occupation sometimes influences coping skills: amongst the families were a doctor, funeral director, nurses, and a policeman, all with a highly developed skill of shielding themselves from stress. I should like to refer to this again, later.

One might therefore define a crisis as an event demanding an emotional response from a person that they are not able to give – the threatened loss of a child is like this and causes parents to feel helpless and vulnerable. It is possible that Mr Long, who became so alienated from the hospital, may have been better able to receive help and support if help had been available at the very beginning. However, he met the demands of the crisis alone, with a reaction of complete denial. With this in mind, Caplan's point is crucial:[4] some intervention at the time of a crisis is vital to enable an individual to cope – intervention may be from friends or family or from an outside agency. When parents are frightening in their distress and despair, it is tempting to delay, but this will be very easily and quickly interpreted as indifference and it is not surprising that hostility and alienation result.

## TOWARDS A WAY OF COPING

Some parents referred to a period between first being told the diagnosis and the time when they felt they were beginning to manage their lives again (Wickens family). It seems to be a period of numbness and complete disorientation. This short section is about helping parents through that period.

Basic necessities have to be provided, and parents may wish for help with this, ensuring that travelling between home and hospital is possible, that the budget can include this as well as all its normal commitments, that arrangements can be made for other children at home to be taken and collected from school and cared for, and that other responsibilities are adequately covered. One parent resented a little this kind of help that was offered to him, feeling it too much of an intrusion into family life, but two others specifically said they were glad of help at this time because it was so difficult to think of anything but the sick child and fares were such a drain on the pocket (Wickens, Kingston).

Having introduced oneself to parents I think a second contact within a few days should be made to see how they are managing and to offer again some time to discuss the treatment schedule, and to emphasize that difficulties within the family do sometimes occur and that one is available specifically to discuss these problems should the parents wish. Depending upon how the interview has gone it may be appropriate to tell the parents that it is helpful just to talk to someone at times, and that other parents have found this – they should not hesitate to come to the social worker's office at any time. The difficulty here is to achieve a balance between encouraging parents to talk and harassing them when they do not wish to, a skill that was admired by some of the parents.

If parents clearly do not wish to talk it is important to accept this and recognize that all that is appropriate has been done. To continue to talk is likely to make the parents feel trapped and resentful and very hesitant to come at some later date. If they do talk, a likely reaction is to express guilt concerning their feeling of personal responsibility in causing the illness – in their care or in failing to get medical attention quickly enough. Reassurance must be given carefully because often it *would* have been possible to have acted more quickly, to have insisted on a second medical opinion or to have taken the child to the doctor more promptly. One parent whose child had many bruises hesitated because of fear of being thought to have abused the child (Mrs Philips). Others delayed because of the doctor's scorn at their fussing. Parents know these delays might have been avoided and quickly to dismiss their guilt with reassurance does not help them to share it or put it into perspective.

A second early reaction is grief and mourning for the healthy, fit child who is lost – the child to whom so many expectations and hopes were attached is gone and replaced by one for whom the future is limited and sorrowful.

'We mourned Mathew (8) the day they told us he had leukaemia' (Wickens).

'He was not the same boy during treatment – it made you wonder if it was worthwhile' (Mr Temple).

The response to drugs is often quick, and remission and subsidence of the symptoms follow – the child may look much better and be discharged to receive treatment as an out-patient. These factors are a cruel boost to the psychological reaction of denial. Parents are tempted to believe that their child will be exceptional: his physical state, better than for a long time, supports this and ideas of a miraculous cure grow (Drew, Kingston). It is very tempting for the social worker too, to collude with this and to share the enthusiasm – to do otherwise smacks of being indifferent to the prospect of a cure or to be depriving the parents of hope, although of course this is not the case. Again one is attempting to achieve a balance between optimism and realism, perhaps biased towards over-optimism, because it is so sustaining and is a way to survive each day.

Friedman suggests explaining that it is a common reaction of parents to feel a diagnosis as serious as leukaemia must be in error because the child looks very healthy after a good response to treatment:

> Often, there is prompt remission which supports any existing parental denial of the seriousness of the illness. Relatives and friends may further reinforce this by pointing out that the child looks too well to be sick or by recalling instances of mistaken diagnosis. The physician can be of great help in such instances by anticipating this and explaining that it is natural for them to find it difficult to believe the diagnosis when their child appears so well. This type of counselling aids the parents in their dealings with relatives and friends and often helps them in resisting the advice to seek medical opinion and management from some other source.[5]

A task that the parents of Damien Drew welcomed my undertaking was informing Damien's teacher and headmistress and those of Damien's brother Gerald. Richard, the oldest boy, was about to begin a training apprenticeship and I spoke also to his personnel manager. This is much more than a telephone task because teachers, especially in Junior and Infant Schools, are likely to be very involved in the lives of their pupils and very shocked by the news. The Drews felt they could not face this task and were very ready for me to do it on their behalf. Mr Thomas said he felt he could manage 'the telling' but would find it hard to cope with the reaction of others that might show great distress. The majority of parents, however, tended to prefer to do any necessary 'informing' themselves.

From the comments of most parents and the direct confirmation of two (Wickens), there is a transition period between the era of normal life and an era that is centred around hospitals and treatment, and lived with a different philosophy – a 'day by day' philosophy. Once an initial contact with parents at the time of diagnosis, that is at the beginning of this period, is made, I feel it is part of the total care of the family and child to follow the first visit quickly with a second. The social worker needs to be available as someone that parents can collapse on and rely on and who will arrange for any practical things to be done that they cannot face whilst they stumble and grope towards a way of being able to cope alone.

## THE TREATMENT PERIOD

In the last two sections I have discussed how parents can be offered help at the time of diagnosis and in the first days and weeks afterwards. In this section I should like to discuss some of the problems parents and children face during the course of treatment until the outcome of the treatment is clear. This normally lasts from between a few months to two or three years.

In the introduction I stated that one of the lessons I had learned had been the special importance of offering help to families in the context of the family's own pattern of coping – that few rules or guide lines could be laid down about giving help. I mention this again here because it seems particularly true for the period covered by this section. Although there are some similarities between families in their way of reacting and adjusting to a fatal illness in one of the children of the family, each family has an individual and dynamic way of coping. With this in mind, this section is about some of the effects of leukaemia on family functioning and on individuals in families.

### The family

Ross describes the effect on a family of an exceptional child from a sociological viewpoint.[6] In this vein I find it useful to imagine the family as a network of relationships. In a straw mobile, when one straw is removed or radically changed, the whole mobile rocks, becoming for a while unstable and precarious and only gradually settling down, with each straw having a new position and role in the structure. Similarly with the family when it is struck by the news of serious illness in one member, a period of instability follows, the family only gradually settling down and each member having new expectations and roles. It is easy to see how weaknesses in the previous family structure lead to adverse family functioning, when special individual needs are created by a crisis. For example, in a family where the mother feels unable to share her anxieties with the father, she may try to share her fear of treatment by explaining to her son in exaggerated detail each medical procedure he will have to undergo; or a son who has a poor relationship with his mother becomes a focus for his mother's anger and despair at the threatened loss of another child. An obvious way for a family to cope is to have an unspoken understanding that the illness is mentioned as little as possible. It can then seem as though a stiffness or tension has descended enveloping the whole family. Turk speaks of family members being caught in a 'web of silence':

> We also need to realise that the Cystic Fibrosis child is frequently aware of the demands he makes on the family. If these demands are not discussed freely, then everyone is caught in a "web of silence" revolving round his own feeling of frustration. This creates a burden for everyone, including the C.F. child, and if not discussed it can impair the psychological functioning of all members.[7]

The child with leukaemia is as susceptible to this web as the one with cystic fibrosis.

During my interviews with parents, if it seemed that a family did not encourage open communication about the illness, it was tempting to assume that here was the 'web of silence', but in trying to assess this more carefully it was very difficult to distinguish between the tendency to avoid all reference to the illness, and concern not to be preoccupied with it to the detriment of living as normal a life as possible. I think this is a very apt demonstration of the importance of the theme of this study — the need to be conscious of individual family ways of coping — of the pitch a family has taken between the extremes of a web of silence and obsessional preoccupation.

Any overt plan of coping as a family seemed rare (with one exception which I describe in the next section), though this may have been missed because in interviews parents spoke very little of the 'middle period' of the illness. Individuals in families were conscious that everyone was facing the same distress and despair and there was an understandable reluctance to impose on each other (Mr Thomas). Some parents said they fluctuated in mood and were able to give and receive help according to these swings. Two sets of parents said other children in the family seemed to know when they could impose, ask questions or play up, but sensed difficult periods and then were restrained (Kingston,

Thomas). One parent commented on the perceptiveness of his ill child. Linda (8) not only knew and understood that the earlier the diagnosis of the disease was made the better, but that if she had been older she would have understood more and would have needed to ask deeper and more searching questions which would have been harder for her (Thomas). Linda's feeling of relief that she was too young to understand may well be one that her parents felt too. How much the feeling was a joint realization is unknown, but that she should make the comment at all is some testimony to the depth of her understanding about the condition.

### Parents

Only one set of parents referred to a spoken decision about how to cope with all the anger and depression they knew they faced:

'We decided from the beginning that we would take it out on each other rather than on the kids – that was our system and we stuck to it but our rows lost us a lot of friends' (Mr & Mrs Rodgers).

One aspect of treatment in leukaemia is that suddenly parents become far less significant in the care of the child – his survival now depends on doctors, nurses and treatment of which they usually have little knowledge. None of the parents mentioned this directly but all in different ways said that they were not told enough about the treatment programme and felt excluded – this was said the most angrily and emphatically by one father, himself a doctor. His anger was not that he was unable to be involved in the medical care; he did not wish to be so, but that he was made to feel the medical care was none of his concern (Doctor Jacobs).

Involvement of the parents in the total team caring for the child is crucial and they must be told about treatment plans and procedures, the purpose of particular drugs and their side effects, and be shown as much consideration as possible about appointment times and treatment schedules. One social worker has spoken of the need for parents to have 'territory' – for example a parents' sitting room, within the hospital, for two reasons: to confirm their right and the importance of their presence in the hospital as part of the caring team: and as somewhere they can go to be alone – to be able to remove themselves from the public eye and collapse inwards from the strain of keeping up an attitude of hopefulness and reassurance before their child.

Sources of grief

Broadly, there seemed to be three main factors that shaped the grief reaction in the parents I spoke to. First, the feelings associated with past pain and loss; second, the perceived expectations of class, culture, and profession; and third, a deep individual reaction that is not simply the product of early life experiences or simply a response to expectations.

The reaction of a father, a police officer, emphasized the significance that the requirements of one's work have in determining coping behaviour. He had been trained to deal with frightening and distressing situations in a formal and controlled way, precluding emotional interference, and this was bound to influence this father in the way he coped. Other parents acknowledged this influence: a trained nurse felt she might have partly adopted skills of professional care and detachment in caring for her daughter (Mrs Thomas). A doctor recognized a similar tendency in his attitude towards his son (Doctor Jacobs).

Some parents spoke spontaneously of plunging into searching intellectual activity as an attempt to gain some understanding of the cause of the illness or at least to rule out some possibilities:

'I read everything – I got books from the library on acupuncture, faith healing, cancer-causing foods, haematology etc.' (Mrs Kingston).

Parents spoke of reading articles and literature and questioning themselves about their responsibility:

'Should I have taken him to the doctor earlier?'

'Should I have insisted on an earlier hospital examination?'

The idea of bad cells in the blood caused even more searching questions:

'I made a pair of sheets and dyed them – Damien slept in these and I wondered if the dye could have affected his blood' (Mrs Drew).

'I dyed my hair when I was pregnant and thought that that had perhaps affected him' (Mrs Mathews).

The urge was to establish some meaning or explanation to eliminate the possibility of divine punishment or personal blame. Some parents were easier to reassure than others, accepting the doctor's statement that nothing they had done could possibly be identified as causal in any way. Medically knowledgeable parents were, of course, less susceptible to such assurance.

A problem that caused many parents concern was how to allow a child to lead as normal a life as possible without exposing him to undue physical risk. Judgement is complicated by the tendency to over-protect as a compensation for 'allowing' the child to become ill. Ross suggests that over-protection takes two forms.[8] One is indulgence: the child is too fragile to cope with being denied anything and indulgence assuages the guilt of bearing a defective child. The other is dominance: a redirection of hostility towards the child for causing so much disappointment and the need to over-demonstrate quality as a mother to compensate for the 'bad' maternal act of producing a handicapped child.

Of course none of the parents made any reference to feelings in precisely this way but occasions of extreme anger were mentioned:

'This lady just kept staring and staring at James – it was really upsetting him – I could have floored her' (Mrs Rodgers).

'Mathew was playing and the lady went on to say, "Well, he does not look very ill".' Mrs Wickens flared up angrily and said 'Well he has got leukaemia' the word being used as a weapon.

I wonder if suppressed anger is released when a chance remark of someone represents parents' own feelings that are too painful to see in themselves. Mrs Rodgers must have been painfully aware that James did look dreadful and Mrs Wickens must have been conscious of how cruelly Mathew's appearance denied his physical condition. Another factor encouraging over-protection was the attitude of friends and relations:

'I cannot understand you letting him out on his bike when he is so ill' and 'Oh go on let him have it, he may not be able to next year' (Rodgers, Wickens).

In practice the problem most often fell to mothers but fathers were conscious of being unable to help at home because of the need to work:

'One of the worst things is having to go to work in the morning when you know he is not too good – but the world has got to carry on and you have got to keep money coming in' (Mr Temple).

The remark of one parent seems to summarize the many and sad consequences to a family:

'Every level of family life is affected – for example you do not feel very much like celebrating each other' (Mr Thomas).

## Brothers and sisters

Reviewing the interviews and some literature on the reaction of brothers and sisters, three responses stand out: fear, jealousy and regression. Fear can arise from two sources. First the perception that the strength and understanding parents once showed is suddenly wavering, so that parents are depressed, bewildered and themselves frightened, must be very frightening to children. Secondly, when children learn of the cause of their parents' distress, fears relating to the illness arise: for very young children, it is that they have caused the illness by an angry wish or some action, while siblings fear that they too may have the illness. Jealousy and resentment occur at the extra attention the sick child gets, and at the fact that parents are now absent for long periods of time visiting the sick child. Resentment is linked to the occurrence of the illness and guilt and remorse after hospitalization often coincide with an improvement in the patient, reinforcing the belief in the effectiveness of wishes. Guilt suppresses resentment, which may duly emerge in a row:

'They each have had parties at home which the other has refused to attend — they often have semi-play fights but on one occasion Philip (16) lost his temper and said to Neil (14), "Get back to hospital where you belong" — Neil was terribly upset' (Anderson).

Yet the very people a child turned to when distressed are now the focus of chronic distress and have little time or emotional resources to try to understand. Indeed, the unusual behaviour of brothers and sisters may be interpreted as deliberately taking advantage of their preoccupation, or further evidence of their own failure as loving parents. Two parents, disturbed by the increasingly difficult behaviour of the four-and-a-half-year-old sister of a child with leukaemia, returned to the social worker who had offered help at the time diagnosis was made, She was able to talk over with these parents possible causes and help them replan their days so that some time could be devoted by at least one parent each day exclusively to the little girl.

Burton contrasts the reactions of older and younger brothers and sisters — younger ones expressing resentment and jealousy more openly, older ones suppressing feelings and being more protective.[9] Older children face the conflict of resenting the extra attention to a sibling but realizing the need for it, and their resentment is inhibited by the knowledge that the extra care is essential. Only two of the families I interviewed had an older and younger child and the contrast Burton draws seemed to apply. In an earlier work she pointed out the vulnerability of small babies in a family with a sick child because of maternal deprivation.[10] Six of the families I saw had children aged one or younger at the time of diagnosis, or had babies born during the course of the illness. It is impossible to get much idea of the effects on these children, especially in the very informal interviews that I had. The Jacobs were very conscious of possible harm to Ian (3½) and tried to include him in all that happened to Edward (1½). In four families, the parents felt they had still been able to devote time and concern to the babies and did not feel they had suffered in any way (Mathews, Anderson, Temple, Rodgers families).

In contrast, Mr Long said, 'Well we were so rushed that Terrence (14 months) just got changed and fed and that was it.' The family is strictly Jewish and after the death of Patricia, Terrence was sent away to relatives for seven days – children are not allowed in the house during this period of mourning. Even in such a situation it is not possible to make an assessment of the emotional impact on Terrence without a much fuller understanding of the whole pattern of their family life.

One of the conclusions of Burton's study on the families of children with cystic fibrosis was that parents talked very little to their well children about the illness.[11] I had the impression with all the families I interviewed that they were conscious of some of the anxieties that the other children had. The dilemma was to decide how much to talk to the children about the illness – how able they were to cope with it and how much talking might merely lead to unburdening themselves on the children. Each family managed the dilemma in its own way, mainly by giving a euphemistic account of the illness, after questioning from the children. But it was clearly difficult enough for parents to think things over clearly in their own minds, let alone put it into words for children, with a balance of honesty and optimism, geared to the child's understanding. Mr & Mrs Temple spoke of fear of over-burdening Michael (12) but they knew that if they simply said Steven would get better and he did not, the children would not trust them again. Two parents said they would be willing to talk if their children asked but I wonder if children are able to make such a request in words about a subject they know is so alarming and upsetting to their parents (Anderson). I think a social worker has a good contribution to make in offering help to parents to work out how their children might be feeling and reacting and what might be said or done to help them. For example, they might be encouraged to devote even a small amount of time in the day to the child so as to give him the opportunity and confidence to express worry by a tentative remark or question that the parent has time to notice and respond to rather than deflecting it, as might happen in the turmoil of other times.

If one message could be picked out from the literature on death and dying it might be the importance of talking more openly about it and the unhealthiness of denial and suppression. The literature I have in mind has been based mainly on observations of adults facing death or coping with loss. It is not necessarily the case that all the conclusions hold for children; nevertheless many of the reasons for trying to emphasise the importance of being more open about dying not only hold true, but are even more relevant for children. An adult has access to a much wider range of people than a child does; his contact with the world is almost entirely sanctioned by his parents. The sources of help for a child are therefore much more restricted and the help his parents can give him is therefore that much more important.

Parents seemed to say unanimously 'No' to any suggestion that a child should be told of the exact nature of his illness when it is first diagnosed — at all costs the child must be protected from this information and doctors seem to have firmly advocated this attitude. As the illness progresses, if there is a deterioration, then there was more readiness to talk 'if the child wanted to — but they never mention it.'

It is too much to expect parents or anyone else to oppose the whole cultural grain of protecting adults from knowledge of illness and absolutely protecting children. But real care of children must demand a real attempt to enable children to prepare for the possibility of dying. A task the social worker might undertake is to help parents express some of their own fears of the child expressing his, and to practice kinds of answers to the questions a child might ask: 'Am I going to die?' 'What happens after you die?' 'Is it going to hurt?' The construction of replies to these kinds of questions can be based on the meanings and concepts a child uses in his questions so that the answers really meet his questions as accurately as possible. Discussions of this nature in the long middle period of an illness, before the possibility of unsuccessful treatment and death becomes a probability and talking is then far too painful, might do much to reduce childrens' darkest fears and enable them to enjoy and develop the life they have:

'Looking back we would have told Neil (14) about the leukaemia — it might have just burdened him more but overall we think it would have made things easier all round' (Anderson).

## THE CHILD WITH LEUKAEMIA

In earlier sections I have talked about the family of the child with leukaemia, how the members cope and how they might best be helped. In this section I should like to concentrate on the child; on some of the feelings and problems he has. Normally the family will be his main support, but of course the social worker can have direct contact with the child and can do a lot to help him directly. This assertion is based on observations of help given to children during my placement and on accounts of help in the literature, in particular by Tina Jacobs on work done with young children in hospital.[1 2]

In this section I shall attempt to discuss how the general theme of this study relates to direct work with seriously ill children. Given that help should not be aimed at a false ideal, such as 'getting the individual to face reality' but should be directed to involve the 'whole person', and to take account of his defences and blocks and ways of coping — how can this be put into practice in working directly with the child himself?

In an article by Binger, it is suggested that it is relevant to be concerned with communicating to the sick child awareness that he may have many things he wants to talk about and a preparedness to listen to these and not be frightened away.[1 3] The way this is done is very personal and individual, but must involve some preliminary work with parents, to get some idea of how much the child understands, what kind of terms and expressions have been used with him, and how much the parents think it appropriate he should know. With this preparation and some frankness with the child, about how difficult and frightening it is for grown-ups as well as children to talk about illness, the social worker is in a much more confident position to deal with questions and anger and fear that the child wants to share. The child will recognize this himself, and be more confident in his turn. Binger points out that whilst an adult may have a variety of people, independent of his family, that he can turn to for help, all a child's relationships are sanctioned by his parents. But if parents are not included in or do not understand or accept the work a social worker is trying to do with their child it is not very likely they will allow the relationship to continue. Thus any direct work with a child (as opposed to help through the family), first requires working with the parents, in order to learn something of the child's stage of understanding, and to involve the parents and work with their guidance and approval.

The time at which a seriously ill child is likely to come to the attention of the social worker is at diagnosis or just after. He will have had symptoms for a little time before being referred to hospital by his G.P. One important determinant of the way he reacts to hospitalization is his previous experience of illness and medical care. For a young child the experience may be completely new and cause only interest. A child coming into his teens, however, is almost certain to have had some direct experience of illness, in himself, in a relative or friend or, if not, at least to have read or seen on T.V. stories connected with illness. If there has already been a serious illness in the family a child might enter hospital for tests in a state of tremendous alarm.

Apart from this last situation it is unlikely that the child would have much idea initially of the actual nature of his illness or that it could be life-threatening. A common explanation to children with leukaemia is that they have a severe form of anaemia – literally true, but quite deliberately deceptive in choice and casual expression of words. I think there are two main sources of anxiety at this early stage that the worker needs to be aware of and ready to help with. There is the prospect of painful and unpleasant treatment and there is often bewilderment about the parents' behaviour. Some preparation for helping with these anxieties is first to get as clear as possible what schedule of treatment will be administered. This must be done in consultation with the consultant and registrar caring for the child, partly because schedules are not identical, but mainly to find out his views and wishes about what and how the patient should be told. This at least puts the worker in a position to answer with some firmness and precision questions from children and to reassure if there are misapprehensions. However awful the schedule looks I feel it is crucial that there should be no attempt to deny parts of the treatment programme, as this is a formula for mistrust and can only lead the child to be aware that the social worker will not share a painful event even in prospect.

To protect Neil (14) from worrying, Mr and Mrs Anderson used to avoid telling him about a hospital appointment for some painful treatment until the last minute. They describe his reaction as very angry. 'I cannot even trust my own parents.' Much smaller children are aware of deception. Sarah Philips (5) was mystified and suspicious as to why she could not eat any food because she was having a blood test. In fact she was having something more complicated that required an anaesthetic.

On the second point, parents in the weeks after diagnosis are likely to be in the depths of despair and helplessness, feeling quite inadequate to meet the ordeal of months of treatment they are convinced will be futile. Mrs Drew felt she could not face Damien (8), and she could not even start to think about treatment, as she just felt she was breaking apart. Many young children seem to regard their parents as invulnerable and omnipotent. Their perception is also very acute and although all the parents said they immediately resolved to conceal their distress and worry, it would be extraordinary acting that achieved this. It is less likely the child will talk about these perceptions because they are so much more difficult to put into words than feelings about practical things. Because of this it is all the more important for the social worker to be conscious of their existence — they are perhaps the seeds of awareness in the child of something much more threatening than has been presented to him. Whether the social worker instigates some mention of parental reaction must depend upon factors like how the parents have coped, whether they are concerned about the child's perception of their behaviour and whether the child shows any obvious concern about his parents' state. The parents in the study all seemed able to face their children and remain fairly composed —

'I was very afraid of going in to see him and breaking down but I did not — it is easier than you think it will be' (Mrs Masters).

In view of this and the probably only recent involvement of the worker, I think it would be inappropriate to do more than suggest to the child that he might be wondering why Mum and Dad have been so upset or so bad-tempered with the other children and to discuss this only if the child seems concerned or picks up the cue.

There are two other aspects that are important, more directly related to the child's age. For the younger child, it is separation from parents through hospitalization; for the older child it is the fear of a long-lasting illness and disfigurement. Complete separation did not take place in any of the twelve families. Some parents took it in turns to sleep at the hospital and all the parents were there during the major part of the day. The harm that can be done to young children through separation is well documented. For the child who is too young to talk, constant reassurance in very basic language and in as many forms as possible may communicate some understanding. If parents are not able to visit regularly, and these would be very unusual circumstances, the social worker might try to do so, so that there is at least one time during the day when the child has someone who is just his — not a nurse or doctor who is for everyone else as well.

Questions concerning duration and disfigurement are bound to occur to the child on a ward where many types of illness are being treated. Periods of time have such different meanings to different children — answers have to be geared as much as possible to use concepts and terms that can be assimilated. Something that might be helpful in reply to a question about 'how long' is:

'The doctors are going to put something into your blood that will help the cells (the good soldiers), fight the bad ones and in twelve weeks time when it is nearly your birthday (or Easter or Christmas), they are going to look very carefully at how the battle is going on and see whether the good soldiers need any more help or any different help.

This is honest — it is not a complete answer but it does attempt to use concepts that the child is familiar with and can grasp. Thus explanations must strike a balance between being complete and realistic on the one hand and taking account of the child's ability to understand on the other.

Disfigurement is much harder to cope with — it is much more directly distressing. From observing children on a paediatric ward, those of six or less seem to take little account of it except with curiosity, but older children are more likely to show repugnance or to tease. Most treatment schedules for leukaemia involve radio-therapy, which after two to three months causes loss of hair. Nothing could be a greater focus for teasing, and even the most self-assured child will be humiliated during the four-to-eight week period necessary for fresh hair to grow. One mother (Anderson) described how her son used to come home from school in tears at the merciless ragging to which he was subjected. A child can wear a wig so that the disfigurement can be disguised but even so feelings are sensitive and the temptation to isolate oneself and to hide away must be strong. Some indication of this was again made by the Andersons:

'Philip did not go to see Neil in hospital — he said he did not like to see Neil. We think he (Neil) was glad of this, he was in such a poor state he did not want to be seen by anyone.

This is a perfectly reasonable reaction that anyone might have, but there is a danger of the reaction hardening into a kind of depression and a reluctance to see anyone that becomes more and more difficult to overcome the longer it lasts. This imposes a strain on parents and drastically limits the potential for the best use of time later on when the child is less ill. Whilst allowing for times when the child quite naturally does not want to mix, I think it is therefore important to encourage, at other times, participation in games and activities on the ward and in normal life at home. The latter is much harder though, because mothers are bound to tend towards overprotection whereas in hospital there is shared responsibility for the child and skilled medical supervision at hand. At home the mother has to rely on her own judgement to achieve a balance between allowing him to live as normally as possible (racing about, cycling, fighting), but not taking unreasonable risks (severe knocks, contact with any children's illness such as chicken pox). It is an extremely difficult balance to reach and is complicated by her own wish that he be with her as much as possible because their time together is limited. On the paediatric ward where I worked there were three school teachers, who were spending far more time with the children than a social worker could hope to devote to group activities and so were much more aware of how the child was behaving in a group with other children – this was true, of course, for nurses also. A weekly staff support group, run by a psychotherapist for all the personnel of the ward but usually including only social workers, teachers and nurses, produced a tremendous feed-back of information about how a child was coping and what particular roles individuals could take to support the child. It is easy, theoretically, to split up 'jobs' on the ward – the social worker is the one who cares for the 'emotional side', the nurse for the 'medical' and the teacher for 'education' – yet if such a demarcation happens in practice so much care and support to the child that might be achieved is bound to be lost.

I have mentioned in the last section how children become aware of the seriousness of illness in a sibling, not through being simply told but by picking up clues (acute anxiety in parents, preoccupation, short temper, physical appearance) and making deductions gradually. I think the same process goes on for the sick child and that two kinds of ideas are learned. These are, firstly, that something radical has happened or is happening to him since he first went to the doctor, to cause everybody to treat him quite differently from the way they used to and from the other children – even his brothers and sisters. Secondly, talking about feeling unwell and about being afraid is not a very good thing to do.

During this process the same kinds of defences that protect any adult will act to protect the child from complete realization or acceptance of what is implied by repeated hospital treatment and the sudden change of attitudes towards him. There are certain to be times, however, when during a particular stressful time in the adjustment of the family or an unpleasant stage of treatment defences are not able to keep out panic and fear. It is at these times, especially, that a child needs help and support. Apart from the difficulty of actually trying to meet these needs there is the problem of being sure to recognize their presentation and creating the opportunity to respond. If the child is already aware that referring to some of the 'things' he wants to talk about is very disturbing to his parents, then what can he do to reduce his distress but try and suppress them or express them in a different form? How then can we help to prevent the fundamental conflict of feelings: 'Something very bad for me is happening. I must not talk or ask about it'?

Tina Jacobs describes work she has done in hospital with very young children, Patty (3) and Maisie (2).[14] She worked with the children directly because for geographical or other reasons she could not help the children through their parents. Miss Jacobs spoke of devoting some individual time, for twenty sessions, to Patty before she felt a sufficiently trusting relationship had been established with the child to begin to encourage Patty to talk about some of her fears. Such long preparatory work may be essential in working with children with leukaemia if a relationship is to be formed in which children are able to talk about some of the feelings that disturb them most. None of the children of the parents I spoke to were separated from their parents as were Patty and Maisie, and of course parents were the primary people in helping the children through illness. But to imagine that parents can talk over with their children treatment plans and always have emotional resources to cope with their own feelings and the child's anxieties is unrealistic. Even in an ordinary family situation, children are inhibited from saying anything that they think will shock, frighten or alienate their parents. It is therefore important to give children the opportunity to talk with someone else, just as parents do, and for at least one identical reason — not wishing to impose painful feelings on someone very close. If this is attempted, however, it is vital that parents understand why it is thought helpful to see the child alone and what kind of things are being discussed in interviews. This is particularly difficult for three reasons. To suggest seeing the child alone is a further take-over from the parents of the care of their child — further exclusion of their participation in his care. It may seem to imply that the parents are not able or competent enough to meet the emotional needs of the child: 'You mean our boy cannot talk to us?' Finally, it smacks of encouraging the child to talk about his illness as though it were a good thing that he should want to talk about it at length.

I think it is easy to become so accustomed to the idea that sharing worrying things is helpful that we forget that the very opposite may seem, and sometimes is, the best thing to do. Ways of sharing and coping are unique in families, and one must get some indication from parents of how the family copes with stress — how, when, and to whom do the children talk about fears and how do the parents respond. The whole theme of this study is the importance of being conscious of the unique way individuals and families cope with stress and fear and of taking this into account in offering help. If this is not done, help offered may seem just absurd, pointless or interfering and then anger and hostility is caused by what is perceived as meddling intervention. It is a basic principle of social work 'to start where the client is', but defences raised in response to threatened loss or to death are so highly pitched that unless an approach particularly conscious of this is used much harm may be done. Yet help *can* be effective. Two parents described how pleased and grateful they were that a psychologist saw their son regularly alone — they were quite aware that this gave Steven the opportunity to share things he did not want to mention to his parents and quite understanding that the relationship had to be confidential and they should not ask what had been discussed (Temple family).

It is certainly not necessary that this kind of counselling should be done by a social worker — a teacher or family friend may have the opportunity to form a much closer relationship. One parent referred to the support given to Christine (11) by the headmistress of the small school she attended, when her younger sister Linda was ill (Thomas family).

Just as quick involvement with the parents is important, so it is with the child when his impressions about the hospital, and the new body of personnel he is meeting, are first being made. Generally, in helping children to talk, it is good to avoid too much questioning as this is so directive of what they are to say. Similarly, too much reference to his feelings about hospitalization may be unwise. If the emphasis can be on giving the *opportunity* to talk and getting across one's preparedness to do so, without *insisting* upon it (for example, by treating seriously and carefully references, even those comically disguised, to the illness), then there is less risk of simply stirring up anxiety that has to

be coped with later by parents at home. Morrisey cites research supporting the value of 'qualitative parent participation', that is, consistent
participation and visiting.[15] It is likely that this holds true for social
worker participation too. Even if visits are short but regular and frequent, this is better than the random long casework-orientated interview.

## Regression

A response often referred to in the literature is regression. For example,
Wolff says:

> One possible psychological mechanism available to the child is
> to give up behaviour patterns appropriate to his age and revert
> to behaviour that gratified him in the past.[16]

But the comments of parents suggests that this is not nearly so
straightforward as it seems from the statement by Wolff. Whilst, in
adversity, it is a natural response for adults to relapse into a partly
helpless state (and sometimes a welcome thing to do), it is not necessarily so for children who have only recently acquired the ability to
be independent in some aspects of their behaviour and are extremely
reluctant to give this up.

The response to hospitalization or over-protection may then be
anger and frustration, just as much for the teenager who feels thwarted
of the complete adult independence that seemed so close at hand, as
for a four- or five-year-old who has just begun to be able to play freely
away from his mother's immediate watchful eye. This provides some
clue to the hatred and hostility that some children have expressed to
their parents (Masters and Anderson families).

A second cause of anger in young children is towards the illness
itself, as though the illness had a mind and was deliberately choosing
to harm the child – the animistic interpretation of phenomena. At
this stage, the child is also egocentric and assumes he must be linked
to the illness in a causative or deserving way, that he is being punished
and his omnipotent parents have failed to prevent the punishment and
are punished in return.

But regression is by no means the only response to be observed.
Five sets of parents said firmly that they thought their child had
matured as a result of being forced to face the fragility of life, of
having to face painful treatment and because of very many more

relationships with adults such as the hospital personnel and private tutors that they had. This factor has not been mentioned in the literature I have seen, but it caused problems to some parents who mentioned the impatience of a child (14) towards his older brother (16) whom he regarded as much less mature (Anderson), and the reluctance of a boy to play with children of his own age, preferring to be with older ones in physically more hazardous games.

No clear pattern relating to regression or increased maturity emerged, but I had the impression, for those children that deteriorated and died, of alternating states of maturity and regression. In the last stages of illness, some children were so psychologically affected that a comparison of their emotional state with that of a healthy child is not possible.

## Age

Sula Wolff cites evidence from an American study, identifying four years as a critical age below which children are much more prone to anxiety and disturbance during hospitalization and after, and for whom the most effective support is the actual presence of their mother. Children older than four were more concerned with the actual nature of the illness and were more susceptible to reassurance about parents.[17]

The expression of anger varied with age, younger children acting out their feelings by refusing to take medication, whilst older children made more use of verbal skills. The refusal of medication is a very effective weapon against parents and nothing could be more alarming than the prospect of long battles with a child over a medicine bottle. But it is important to be cautious in reaction to this and not simply to attempt to reason and cajole and warn the child of the seriousness of his illness, as this may be the very reason he refuses the medication, in an attempt to deny its seriousness. Unless it is judged to be simply a piece of playing up, a more sensitive approach would be to help the child talk about the illness, its cause, its effect on him for the future and on the family and help him with fears he has in these areas. Some knowledge of the flexibility of drug schedules would be helpful, and of course consultation with a child psychotherapist or psychiatrist if refusal persists.

In accordance with the theme of the study the main point that should be made is the importance of being available and prepared to talk with patients and their families rather than seeking for general principles of what is right and wrong to do and say.

As an exception to this it does seem important to talk to children directly about the illness and its treatment. Neil Anderson (14) was the only child reported to have referred to this but he did so forcibly: 'I am never asked about anything that is done to me at hospital.' Green supports this:

A child's belief that his doctor will always try to tell him what is going to happen probably does more than anything else to foster complete trust in the physician. The child's active role in the management of his illness is enhanced by unhurried, honest, factual explanation of the disease and its treatment. These discussions need not be complete in every detail but sufficient for him to feel at least partially in control of his situation. Such presentations are reassuring rather than upsetting.[18]

## THE OUTCOME OF TREATMENT

There are several possible outcomes to treatment: a successful stable remission, and termination of treatment; relapse and initiation of a further programme; deterioration and death. I will concentrate in this section on the latter outcome.

I would like to discuss the comments parents have made with regard to their own feelings, those of the sick child and those of the brothers and sisters in the last weeks of illness. I also want to compare some of these comments with points made in the literature and to pick out some aspects of individual ways of coping. Several of the situations I describe in this section illustrate the importance of social workers resisting the urge to intervene in order to 'improve' or change coping behaviour, especially when this urge arises from a desperate desire to do anything rather than nothing in an extremely painful situation. 'I *must* find a way to get Freddy to talk about what it is like to have all this painful treatment.' A more important concern than talking is perhaps availability and preparedness to talk. Parents spoke highly of the social worker with whom they were able to establish a relationship that did not continually question or persuade them to share their feelings, but allowed them to approach the social worker at any time and expect to be heard quickly if not immediately.

### The coping of parents

In the seven families of which I had knowledge where a child had died, it seemed to have become clear by the last few weeks of life that there was very little hope and nothing further that could be done towards cure. Several parents spoke of the importance of never giving up hope, of the need for their own sake to believe right until the end that there was still a chance 'or you will never carry on' (Masters, Kingston, Rodgers).

Corresponding to the doctors' awareness of the fruitlessness of further treatment, some parents also had to change their expectations, although most were fully aware of the prognosis. Decisions by doctors, relating to the appropriateness of continuing treatment in these situations of terminal illness, seem to be taken over a period of time, partly through discussion but partly via a kind of unspoken understanding between doctors. Perhaps this is because of the inherent painfulness of such a decision. If a good relationship exists between the doctor and social worker the latter can be included in the decision and how it is conveyed to the parents. He is then in a much better position to offer help to parents, struggling with their great ambivalence regarding the continuation or termination of treatment. Social workers, for all their ability in relationships, are not renowned for those they have with doctors, but without some common understanding the chances of a jointly considered approach to the family are nil. I think also that the arrival of a definite time when attempts at treatment are curtailed is a psychological aid to the family in the grieving process – it allows a more open contemplation of the loss of a member without the restraint of 'hoping and not letting oneself think about death or the possible failure of treatment.'

If the child is in hospital at the time this decision is gradually formed, parents may be able, or encouraged, to take him home with the back-up of a health visitor and an assurance that he can be brought back directly to the ward without having to go via a G.P. or an outpatients department. It is a dilemma for parents to know exactly what to say to the brothers and sisters of a sick child about his illness and its deterioration. On the one hand they do not wish to overburden them by being too frank – on the other they are concerned not to deceive them lest the children, on knowing of the deception, are mistrustful of their parents' assurances about their own health. There is little basis for supposing children less able to bear the prospect of loss than adults, but the two adults on whom children depend most for support are likely to be in a poor state to offer reassurance and comfort. The parents themselves are, however, likely to have many more outside contacts on whom to lean and rely. There is an interesting contrast between two sets of parents who took opposite courses:

Mary (7) asked if Johnny (20 months) might die; the Kingston's replied to this fairly straightforwardly: 'He might die but we are all doing everything possible to make him well – he has got a good appetite and he is a strong boy so everything is in his favour'. They prayed together for him ... they tried to include Mary as much as possible by making her part of 'the three of us who are caring for Johnny' to keep her involved as much as possible.

This child seems to have been told quite fully, but Michael (12) and Brian (6) were not told at all that Steven (9) might die – only that he had a severe anaemia. After Steven's death, Michael was quite angry that the seriousness of Steven's illness had been kept from him but said he understood his parents' motivation and agreed that he would have worried and he would not have been able to treat Steven naturally (Temple family).

A different approach was taken to these two children but they behaved very similarly after their brothers' death. This is only one example but it does suggest that it is not possible to simply say 'yes, telling the children is best' or 'no, to protect them from the truth'. Coping behaviour in families is unique and complicated and cannot be subject to a broad generalization of 'what is best'.

The last weeks are an ordeal in which meticulous nursing care is required. There may be struggles, hours long, to stop nose bleeds when blood will not clot, trying to hold ice cubes to the nose, adding further stress to an already desperate relationship. The illness and side effects of drugs have disabling and distressing effects: paralysis of limbs, loss of sight, regression or an emotional state akin to senility. Parents spoke of wondering each day whether 'this would be the day', of gradually losing patience with the people who kept coming in asking 'How was he?' when there was no change, or if there was, it was not to be talked about in front of the child. A more awful ordeal for parents to survive is hard to imagine.

Yet it was heartening to hear in each interview how parents did survive, managing to remain calm when with the child, managing to answer difficult questions, to respond to the odd things the child might say in a reassuring way, to cope with hostility and resentment. One parent described how he responded when his child, aged eight, in hospital a short time before he died, said 'take me out of here'. Without of course anything actually happening, he talked to the child as though he were leading him down a corridor and through a door at the end leading out of the hospital – 'Are you through now? O.K.' The child was able to answer he was and, shortly after, died. It must be difficult for parents to be sure of exactly what they have said to children near the end but it sounds as though this child might have received a lot of support from his father in his fear of death (Wickens family).

Two parents described how a friend in hospital, whose child had died, said he did not really feel the child was *his* child – behaviour and appearance had been so altered. Whether this was a sudden reaction or part of a long process of 'anticipatory mourning' (described in texts as emotional distancing enabling parents to contemplate and begin to prepare for loss) is unknown, but the parents said they too had this feeling as their son deteriorated – he had become another person (Wickens family).

Attitudes and feelings about how worthwhile treatment was varied between parents and at different stages in the illness. Nearly all the parents in each case, in the same way, said that hope must never be given up. Mr Rodgers and Mr Temple, whose children had both died, questioned whether the treatment and its failure was worth the changes caused in the child and the pain he suffered.

Of two mothers, one said, at the time treatment was having good effects on her son, that should he relapse when treatment ceased she would rather he die than go through the whole schedule again. Another at the time her son relapsed, was determined treatment should start again and immediately. Warnings that children did not respond so well after one relapse were dismissed by her: 'there has to be a first time' (Mrs Masters, Mrs Kingston).

Clearly, from the questioning of the two fathers above, but also from all the parents, mothers seemed much more positive and enthusiastic about treatment and more optimistic. Maybe this is a reflection of the much greater involvement mothers had in the direct care of their children. If so it is an important indicator of the link between the involvement of parents and their confidence in the medical care of their child.

A question social workers are likely to face and about which three sets of parents spoke was 'Why *my* child – what has he done to harm anyone?' (Wickens, Rodgers, Kingston). Only one couple said they had received a satisfactory answer, from a vicar who had called by chance and began to visit regularly. He suggested that the question implied: 'Why not that rotten little spoilt kid down the road?' and that with this implication, would the parents still ask the question? Is leukaemia something that some children deserve more than others? He went on to say that some families and children seem to have special capacities and qualities which help them to bear a critical illness or handicap. These comments may be regarded with cynicism or contempt by some but they did mean a lot to the parents and held value where the words of others sounded empty (Rodgers family).

Other parents spoke of the courage and fortitude their children showed and spoke with similar words to those of the vicar. They took comfort from the idea that their child was especially well endowed to be able to cope. To some extent the question assumes logic and reason behind the selection of one child to become ill, disregarding the doctors' affirmations that the occurrence is completely by chance. It is reassuring to establish some cause and if it is not organic it must be divine: punishment following a deed for which guilt must be felt. Sometimes, talking about the need to find a cause might help parents to realize the fruitlessness of such a task and so save them the anguish of searching their lives for misdeeds. That it is fruitless I am sure, for what more can a labelled cause be than a focus for blame that blocks coping and grieving processes.

All the parents commented on the importance of living day by day. Another observation from all parents but one was the relief when the child died. This stemmed from two main feelings: relief that the child had to suffer no more, and the exhaustion of parents who were at the end of their own resources, especially when the child had struggled on for longer than the doctors had predicted.

Much of the literature discusses the guilt parents feel at this relief. I am sure this may be so but none of the parents referred in any way to such a feeling. It is unlikely it did not exist and so perhaps parents were reluctant to speak of it — again a point important to note in working with parents, as unresolved guilt is such a restraint on grieving and undermines faith in oneself as a worthwhile person capable of loving relationships. The last stages of illness can be extremely frightening and some parents, having taken their child home to die, may return him to hospital, unable to continue his care at home. They know he fears and dreads hospital and may well be overcome with remorse. Lily Pincus notes,

> The lay person must care for and understand the bereaved and offer him the degree and quality of compassion and reliability which will enable him to regain hope. Only then when this has been achieved can he risk a new attachment.[19]

The coping of children

Nurses and social workers have both spoken to me of the awareness of death they know many terminally ill children have. Two sets of parents added weight to this in speaking of the deaths of their own children. One I referred to above, where Mathew Wickens asked his father to help him out of the hospital. The other couple did not think Jim (8) was aware at all, yet he seemed prepared. In his last week he gave away toys that previously he would never even share, on his last night he told his father not to bother with the early morning drink he usually brought in, and he said he would not return to the school, which he loved. This awareness has been noted in adults too by Cecily Saunders, who believes the awareness comes from the processes of the illness, from past experiences with others who have died and from careful observations.[20] In children I would say that the latter factor is of over-riding importance. But if parents have taken the view throughout the illness that the child must not be told, I do not see that the social worker has any basis for doing other than supporting the parents in these wishes. One cannot simply say 'it would be better for the child to know' — such a judgement has to be made in the context of the whole pattern of family communication and coping and the child cannot be split away and considered independently of the relationships linking him to his family. Pressure on reluctant parents to be frank with their child might cause far more distress to the child through the anguish he perceives in his parents. Outside pressure to communicate and cope in a way quite inconsistent with and alien to the family pattern could cause distress to everyone. 'It would have been just too much — I think he would have broken up if we had said anything' (Wickens family). One can quote many examples when what should be said or done by parents seems easy and obvious from outside the family. My contention is that it is very easy for social workers to fail to take account of unique family patterns of coping and to offer help simply on the basis of ideal ways of coping: 'you must accept and come to terms'. Simon Olshansky refers to this in an article on chronic sorrow as a response to having a mentally defective child:

> When the parent is asked to 'accept' (mental deficiency), it is not clear just what he is being asked to do. The great stress professional workers tend to place on 'acceptance' may suggest to the parent that he is expected to perceive his child from the point of view of the professional helper.[21]

We must strive to see the child from the point of view of his family and in the context of his family life. One feels desperate to intervene to help in some way, any way, to alleviate the situation. The great danger is that we alleviate the pain of our own impotence at the cost of attempting to impose an alien way of coping. One hears of situations when dying children have asked parents if they are going to die and have been assured to the contrary. It is not fair to say 'It would have been better to be honest, or face reality'. At this final stage, parents and children have to muster all the resources they can to survive psychologically. Maybe denial is a way in a particular relationship of actually confirming the imminence of death and a method of coping with it.

The combination of the illness and an accumulation of side effects of drugs can cause children to behave in a bizarre way with wide swings of mood, at times refusing to talk or even to notice people's presence: One boy wandered on the ward, picking up telephone receivers and listening – searching for some reassurance that no one could give. How does one act with children in the last stages of illness? I felt the dilemma in visiting a child (9) in his last week, who was quite normally conscious but very frightened and short tempered. Damien was propped on a settee watching T.V., a continuous nose bleed being mopped by his mother. Probably the best thing was to sit and enjoy the programme with him – something genuine. Talking was inevitably going to create a 'double bind' with its transparent cheerfulness.

Sylvia Anthony has examined the origins of death anxiety in children and notes fear of separation as a primary factor in children of at least four.[22] This might be why children sometimes wish their parents to die with them. Constant reassurance in as many forms as possible has been advocated for young children in hospital separated from their parents and I think the same holds for children facing death who are also bewildered and afraid.

## The coping of brothers and sisters

The parents referred mostly to the reaction of brothers and sisters after the death of the child. There was some suggestion that they were aware of the deterioration, from parental behaviour, just as they were aware of the seriousness of the situation at the time of diagnosis. Michael Temple (12) told his parents after Steven died that he had become gradually afraid to come home from school in case there was a note pinned on the back door to say they had rushed off to hospital. Mary

Kingston (7) knew John's condition was linked to his appetite and the significance of this fading in the last weeks. There was much variation in what and how brothers and sisters were told when a child died, depending for example on time and place of death and how much the parents had talked with them about the illness during its course. Two sets of parents explained to their other children (7) and (4 & 2) that John and James had died in the night, by saying Jesus had taken them and now they were safe and happy with him in heaven. This worked for the moment but caused worries later. 'Supposing Jesus decides to take me or mummy or daddy?' Mary (7) slept badly and seemed distracted. She became acutely alarmed if her father was at all late from work. Mary's mother guessed the cause of her alarm and was able to reassure her that Jesus had taken John only after he had been very very ill and Mary, Mummy and Daddy were all well and Jesus certainly was not going to take them. Rosenblatt describes a very similar reaction in a boy (6½) to the death of his sister (2½). Martin was very afraid that God might take him too if he needed an extra angel or as a punishment for wishing his sister dead for continually pestering him and taking his toys. Just a few sessions in which he was encouraged to share his fears and given reassurance that 'wishing' did not 'cause' helped Martin.[23] Some distinction between parental punishment and the kind of divine biblical punishment is important, but this is an area for specialized expert help.

Bowlby has referred to three types of reactions of children to loss – anxiety, and the anger and distress of both hope and despair.[24] Brian Temple (6) reacted in all these ways when his brother died, but for short spells only. His ability to return quickly to normal behaviour provided the only thread of continuity and gave comfort to the family. His elder brother Michael (12), even a year later, still initiates long discussions at bedtime about the illness. He is very concerned about how parents cope who do not have any religion to support them and I wondered if this reflected his own doubts. Brian also wanted to talk and was concerned with whether the disease was hereditary. His mother was pregnant and perhaps his fear was two-fold – of the illness striking him and of losing the coming baby.

It was clearly very important and valuable to these boys that their parents were prepared to talk to them, not only helping them understand but indicating that the subject could be talked about and demonstrating their confidence in the value of this.

## Coping after death

Just as the shock of diagnosis affected every level of family functioning, so too did the death of a child. Mr Temple spoke of a wound to his family that he felt would never heal. Both parents in the family said the worst times were when you suddenly remembered the loss, you spoke to a friend of 'my three children' and then did not know how to correct yourself. Other parents mentioned anniversaries and objects that reminded them – birthdays and Christmas, toys and clothes. Two parents spoke of the difficulty of getting accustomed to the idea that the child would never be back in the house. Both these parents took some comfort from a belief in a continued existence: one in heaven, the other in the possibility of reincarnation (Kingston, Wickens families).

Some parents spoke bitterly or angrily of the delay in getting practical help – 'everything always came just too late'. Of course there is great inertia in the provision of services, but the way the feelings were expressed suggested a projection of distress about the shortness of life.

Relief at death was certainly present, but to give up a whole pattern of life centred around the sick child was not always easy. A social worker spoke of a mother who was not able to give up the ritual of coming to the ward each day after her child had died, and came, presenting photographs of him lying in his coffin. The habit of attendance at hospital and daily administering drugs is a ritual so strongly linked with the survival of the child that in extreme cases it cannot be abandoned, because it would mean acknowledging the death at too deep a level.

Just as the final help that could be offered to the sick child was reassurance, so it is with the family after his death – reassurance that the strength and intensity of feelings they have is normal, that obsessional retelling of all the details of death, feeling detached, remote from oneself, numb (depersonalization) were not signs of madness. If parents can be encouraged and reassured not to struggle to stifle these feelings with feverish mental or physical activity they may be able to let themselves more fully experience the grief and embrace the pain as a means to a deeper adjustment towards living a life without the child.

It seems that in families where there have been particular stresses in relationships, suppressed during a child's illness, these re-appear, compounded with grief and despair. Normal bereavement reactions of indifference and apathy further limit resources, already inadequate for resolving conflict. Individual family members blame themselves and each other for the death; for failure to approach a doctor early or insistently enough; for the difficult behaviour of one child that allegedly prevented parents giving enough attention to the sick child and so on. It is difficult in these circumstances to know how to focus help, as relationship problems become masked by bereavement reactions. If work with the family continues, a point must be reached when it becomes necessary to say that problems in coping have their roots in the family situation before the loss of their child, rather than in bereavement itself. To continue seeing a family where this seems to be the case when they assume one's involvement is to help them with their loss cannot be justified indefinitely. Making a distinction between grief reactions and the family's earlier relationships is partly artificial; nevertheless it may have to be made if help is productive and not merely an act of collusion in masking relationship problems. I do not underestimate the difficulty of doing this for someone who has been involved with the family throughout the child's illness, because it may seem so much like adding unnecessarily to family stress. It may therefore be helpful for a different worker to become involved.

With many everyday situations in which a social worker is involved individuals or families are familiar with the situation and are coping to some extent. Any intervention, designed to offer alternative ways of coping, can be easily resisted because the urgency to adapt or change is not great. The situation of a fatally ill child is so unfamiliar and the need to find some way of surviving the ordeal psychologically intact is so urgent that the potential for influence by the social worker is much greater (one of the principles of crisis intervention). This, together with the social worker's own anxiety to intervene, leads to the theme of this study, that special care has to be taken to resist the temptation to try and intervene to force parents into ways of coping that seem comfortable and familiar to the social worker, but which ignore the family's own management methods and defences. I have tried to demonstrate some of the ways families have coped with the loss of a child and to initiate thoughts about intervention that is conscious of the pressure to 'do something' and of the importance of relating help to the parents own ways of coping.

## CONCLUSION

The purpose of my conclusion is to summarize briefly some of the main points that parents made in the interviews. The most outstanding of these is an almost unanimous feeling of lack of inclusion in the care of the child — failure to be told basic aspects of treatment like schedules, side effects of drugs, response to treatment — and this often caused resentment and alienation. Many parents emphasized the value and importance of financial and practical support but complained that this was very slow in coming if available at all. Parents also spoke of the need to adopt a new philosophy of life in order to survive — the 'day by day' philosophy that helped them and their child to derive as much as possible from each day without its being over-shadowed by the prospect of what tomorrow might bring.

Five of the eleven sets of parents interviewed had not had any contact with a social worker. It was interesting that the general feeling amongst the five seemed to be surprise at the suggestion of social work help, with responses like: 'What on earth could they do?' One parent, who had expressed the most surprise, nevertheless said at the end of the interview that it had been very helpful to talk: 'You know I've been saying all along that an outsider couldn't do anything, but it's been worth it to talk it over — it does help and it's not too hard' (Mr Philips).

Of the six sets of parents who had received help, all were enthusiastic, and the main criticism was the social worker's lack of time to devote to longer interviews or more frequent ones. The contrast certainly emphasizes the importance of quickly seeing parents after diagnosis, before they have become too alienated, either because they feel they need some help and no appropriate help is forthcoming or because they have closed the barriers to it because of their impression that those caring for their child are indifferent to or unconcerned with the needs and distress of his parents.

Finally, I have been very conscious of the absence of any direct feed-back from children themselves and think this should be essential to any further study of the nature of help that can be given to children having a terminal illness.

### REFERENCES

1. Alan O. Ross, *The Exceptional Child in the Family*, Grune and Stratton, 1964.
2. Margaret Robinson, Family Reaction to Stress, *Medical Social Work Journal* No. 22, 1969.
3. Gerald Caplan, *Principles of Preventive Psychiatry*, Tavistock Publications, 1964.

114 *Children with Leukaemia*

4. Gerald Caplan, op. cit.
5. S. B. Friedman *et al.*, Care of the Family of the Child with Cancer, *Paediatrics*, Vol. 40, Part III, 1970.
6. Alan O. Ross, op. cit.
7. J. Turk, Impact of Cystic Fibrosis on Family Functioning, *Paediatrics*, Vol. 34, 1964.
8. Alan O. Ross, op. cit.
9. Lindy Burton, *The Family Life of Sick Children*, Routledge and Kegan Paul, 1975.
10. Lindy Burton, ed., *Care of the Child Facing Death*, Routledge and Kegan Paul, 1974.
11. Lindy Burton, op. cit.
12. Tina Jacobs, Casework with the very young child in hospital, in *Communicating with Children*, ed. Eileen Holgate, Longman, 1972.
13. C. M. Binger *et al.*, Childhood Leukaemia — Emotional Impact on Patient and Family, *New England Journal of Medicine*, Vol. 280, Part 9, 1969.
14. Tina Jacobs, op. cit.
15. J. Morrisey, Children's Adaptation to Fatal Illness, *Social Work* October 1963.
16. Sula Wolff, *Children under Stress*, Allen Lane, The Penguin Press, 1973.
17. Sula Wolff, op. cit.
18. M. Green, Care of the child with a long term, life threatening illness, *Paediatrics*, Vol. 39, No. 3, 1967.
19. Lily Pincus, How to Help the Bereaved, *Social Work Today*, 2.10.75.
20. Cicely Saunders, The Management of Terminal Illness, *Social Work Today*, 20.2.75.
21. Simon Olshansky, Chronic Sorrow; a Response to having a Mentally Defective Child, *Social Casework*, Vol. 43, No. 4, April 1962.
22. Sylvia Anthony, *The Discovery of Death in Childhood and After*, Allen Lane, The Penguin Press, 1971.
23. B. Rosenblatt, A Young Boy's Reaction to the Death of his Sister, *Journal of American Academy of Child Psychiatry*, Vol. 8, Part 2, 1969.
24. J. Bowlby, *Attachment and Loss*, Vol. II, Basic Books, 1973.

# Face to Face
# with the Unthinkable

ROD BALLARD

I am sitting in front of an electric fire in a large house in a place called Romsey. It is very late at night. Everyone else has gone to bed. The television has closed down, there is nothing on the radio and I am feeling restless and fidgety. This is not really very surprising since Midge, my wife, is over at the hospital having a baby. It started about four hours ago. She began getting pains at regular intervals which is what we had been told to expect and I telephoned the doctor to say what was happening. We got a suitcase already made up with a list of things and we took it over to the hospital feeling rather like a couple of kids going for an outing and hoping that we had remembered everything which we were told would be needed.

I have to admit that I am a bit apprehensive about this whole scene. We have not been married long and the pregnancy was unexpected. We are only twenty-two and prospects are shaky, to say the least. I have at last managed to get a place at college to read for a degree in sociology. I am to start next week. But we have nowhere to live, despite our efforts to buy a house and this is causing a lot of worry. We are of course hugely lucky to have the back stop of a warm welcome from my father-in-law, who has kindly let us get started with the baby in his own home. But I have this feeling of being in someone else's house and whilst there is no real problem about this I would much prefer to be in our own place.

I am not very sure that I am doing the right thing reading for a sociology degree. Above all I am worried about not being able to manage the academic aspect, for I have a penchant for failing exams. Everyone at school thought I was stupid and would never make the grade to higher

115

education. I have had the satisfaction of proving them wrong but always I have a fear of failure. Midge seems confident, however, and I draw a peculiar sense of satisfaction from that.

And now I am waiting for this baby to be born. Neither of us knows anything about babies. When Midge found she was pregnant I rushed out and bought some books about them and we looked at the pictures and read a bit about it all.

Her pregnancy seems to have gone well. We had a hot drawn out summer in a flat near Regent's Park. Me doing an extraordinarily boring job in a records office in some big steel company. A stop-gap between studies. We used to walk in the park and visit the zoo and drink coke on the grass and Midge got tired carrying this baby on long trips around London.

Suddenly the phone rings. I start up from the chair in which I have been sitting and glance at the clock. It is 2 a.m.! Idiot! I must have fallen asleep despite my determination to stay awake and wait for the call.

'Mrs Ballard has had a lovely baby boy,' says a voice.

Relief. She — they — must be alright.

'Can I come and see them?' It's really happened. Now there are three of us.

'It's very late'.

'Please!'

'Well ... alright then'.

I walk across to the hospital which is only 200 yards away. There is a feeling of excitement and expectation for I am going to see a new person who Midge and I have created together and it is all going to be alright. There is a curious sort of awareness of the objects and things around as I walk along. I notice a man going down the road and think to shout to him that I have just been made a father, but decide not to. He will think I am quite mad, talking like that so late at night, so I let him pass feeling sympathetic towards him because he does not know my news.

This feeling of euphoria gives way to some apprehension as I approach the hospital, for I always feel ill at ease in the antiseptic atmosphere that these places seem to generate. I wonder where I have to go. There is no one about to ask and I am worried about going into the wrong room. But I have some vague memory of the place from a former visit. The labour ward must be through here on the right and down the corridor.

There is Midge sitting up in bed having a cup of tea. And a pink warm snuffly baby beside her. She seems very together and composed — almost as if nothing much had happened. She must be so relieved that it's all over. Everybody is very nice. I am offered a cup of tea. The baby looks fine. His little pink tongue flicks in and out and I wonder if that is what all new babies do. I ask Midge and she doesn't know. The whole business is very awe-inspiring and I feel as if we are all going together on some trip into the unknown.

We talk about a possible name but get nowhere, and it doesn't matter at all. I look down into the cot. The baby looks all sort of hunched up as though he has no shoulders. Just his little head sticking out of a huge white blanket. I ask to get a better look and Midge says she thinks it will be alright if I undo it a bit. This reveals his hands which look all sort of papery and five perfect fingers with beautifully manicured nails. What absolute and complete perfection!

It seems that everyone thinks it would be a good idea if we all got some sleep, especially Midge, who I am sure needs it. The baby has his eyes open and seems very contented. He is just one hour old now and perhaps he needs a rest too after all the drama of being born. I kiss Midge goodbye, say goodnight to the staff who smile nicely and seem pleased that I sat up to wait for this event after all.

Back at the house I find it hard to get to sleep. I feel confused but basically at peace. It's such a relief to know that everything is alright. I realize now that I have had stupid ideas in the past about things going wrong which I did not really allow myself to talk about. What a fool. I need not have worried after all.

So with these happy thoughts in my mind I drift off to sleep with a whirl of nurses in white and green and the smell of hospitals and the sight of my new family being put together all passing through my head like so many half-believed events and happenings recurring at times in my dreams.

The next day I am up early, feeling refreshed and rested. I dawdle over breakfast, since I realize I am going to be thoroughly bored for the next few days and very much at a loose end until they emerge from hospital. I am unable to concentrate on the *Times*, which is spread out against the marmalade jar. I read a paragraph or two and realize that I have not taken in a single idea which I can recall. All I want to do is to visit and see them again in daylight and to find out about how the next stage is going. I have heard that women often get depressed after giving birth and I must make quite sure that Midge has all the support

I can get to her. This may mean standing up to the nurses and so on, but it worked last night on the phone so I will try and see if they will let me visit more often, and stay longer when I do.

At last the time comes for me to go over again. There are many more people around and I start off down the same corridor. Someone sees me and says I am not allowed down this one so I turn round and walk the other way, having been directed to the proper place. They must have moved her.

I see a nurse who looks as though she might be a sister. She is dressed in dark blue and has one of those upside-down watches pinned to her bosom. I ask where Mrs Ballard is and she indicates a ward door, and I smile and thank her. But her face remains wooden.

'Are you Mr Ballard?' she asks.

'Yes,' I say, puzzled though not surprised by her manner. This is one of your trained, professional people who have no idea about how to be human to visitors. I make for the door but she calls me back.

'He's going to be a very difficult child, you know'. Hold it. What does she mean? What *can* she be saying? What on earth is she on about? I really can't believe that you can tell what a child is going to be like just after he has been born. The whole thing is preposterous.

'You see he's got those pink little cheeks. Come along.'

She walks past me without a word and leads on through the doors and into the ward. Midge is right at the end and I have to walk down a long line of beds with other mums in who stare at me curiously as I go. Her eyes are red with crying and she is clutching a sopping wet handkerchief.

'What's the matter?' I ask. I was right. This must be the depression emerging already.

'Go on,' I say, not knowing how to begin and feeling thoroughly upset myself at the sight of her like this.

'They say he is going to be handicapped,' she blurts out and looks at me pleadingly, as if asking me to do something about it.

'What do you mean?'

'He's a mongol'.

'A *what*?' I don't know where I am at all now. I think something ghastly has happened.

'I've seen them on buses going to Southampton. They look all peculiar'.

Oh my God. I think I am beginning to understand. This is turning into a nightmare. I don't really want her to go on. The prospects are terrifying.

'Who told you?'

'Dr Rankin. He just came in and said that he was one, and then went away again.'

'You mean he didn't say anything else?'

'No. He came in with someone else but didn't say who, and stayed a couple of minutes and then just turned round and went.'

I sit down on her bed and we hold hands. The other mums look on. I wish we were away from this antiseptic place. I go over and look at the baby but can't see anything different from all the others. How on earth can they tell so early? I am sure there has been a mistake. But Midge seems convinced enough. I ask if she needs anything. She says she doesn't. We just sit, miserable and very frightened.

A nurse announces to all the other visitors that it is time to go. I stay put but she advances across the ward and asks me to leave. Her face is blank and expressionless. I want to ask if I can stay longer but the stuffing has been knocked out of me. I get off the bed and kiss Midge goodbye, thinking that this is absolutely crazy. I've got to leave her behind to be all on her own. I feel angry and very upset. I wonder in a futile sort of way how it is that people can behave in such a stupid fashion. Not a glimmer of understanding appears in the woman's face. I walk away from Midge who starts another bout of crying.

I walk back along the path towards the house, and as I go I look up at the clouds which seem strangely different. Nothing in fact seems the same. I watch the cars going by, their drivers completely oblivious of what has happened to us. I kick a stone and it flies away like one would expect it to. But somehow it should do something different. I feel detached and outside myself. What can it all mean? What did we do?

When I get in I say what has happened to various of my inlaw relatives. They are totally disbelieving and offer reassurance which has a hollow ring. Like me they want the information to go away. I begin to have all sorts of ridiculous ideas about it. I wonder whether it is worthwhile going on for all of us. In some ways it would have been easier if he had been born dead. But this is madness and I feel bad to have these painful thoughts which I try and dismiss as being totally wrong.

So that night I go to bed full of worry and anxiety about our new situation. Life will never ever be normal again. We will have the problem when we are old people. Our blunted lives stretch forward for ever and ever. There can be absolutely no escape.

In no time I am awake. I look at my watch and to my surprise it is quite late in the morning. Something is wrong but for a few seconds I can't think what. Then suddenly the full horror of yesterday floods back. I lie thinking for half an hour, going through the thing over and over again. Someone brings a cup of tea. I find myself saying good morning in a surprisingly cheerful voice. Then I get up and go downstairs for breakfast, and after it is over I find it is time to visit again. When I arrive in the ward Midge seems more cheerful. We don't talk very much. The baby seems to have slept well and is perfectly alright in the sense that he has had a feed and so on. One of the girls next door to Midge has now had her baby. She is surrounded by glowing people, all cooing and chuckling over the new arrival, as pleased as punch. We feel jealous. How lucky they are to be so normal and ordinary.

We spend a miserable few days in this stupid limbo situation, with me visiting and Midge getting about more. Once the sister complains that Midge seems to be crying a lot. Stupid woman. Of course there are tears. I bet she would cry if she had this to cope with. Then, after about a week or so, Midge says one day that she is coming out. This is a fabulous relief.

When they arrive we take the baby out of his cot and put him on the bed and he lies there sleeping contentedly. We decide then and there to call him James, since we are sure that this is a nice name. Then I suddenly remember that I have an uncle called James. Will he mind a mongol being called after him? Well, if he does I will never speak to him again.

Comes the time to change his nappy. Midge approaches tentatively. He is so terribly small. His nappy looks vast round his tiny body. I am anxious that the huge safety pin will prick him, but all is done easily enough. Then begins feeding. He wakes at night. We feel tired next morning. Then he needs feeding and changing again. Gradually a routine builds up. The health visitor says he has a very dry skin and prescribes oiling with some baby lotion.

When Midge was in hospital an appointment was made with a local paediatrician. She has seen no-one other than nursing staff since the G.P. told her that James was a mongol. We go along to his surgery and wait for some time. Then we are asked into his room. He gives us a perfunctory greeting and asks Midge to undress James, which she does under his watchful gaze. She is trembling a bit as she complies. This man makes no attempt whatsoever to acknowledge our feelings of apprehension and fear. He takes one of James' hands and starts putting biro marks all over the palm. I ask him what he is doing and he says, jokingly, that he is taking up palmistry. Ha. Ha! What a joke. I feel absolutely sick with the man. Then he takes each of James' legs and works them up and down.

Eventually he announces that the baby is definitely a mongol. He says he will be very backward and won't make the milestones in a normal way. He does not make opportunities for us to ask questions. The whole session lasts about ten minutes. We leave thinking that this must be a very busy man with no time to spend with the likes of us. We feel stupid, and the whole exercise has been rather frightening and very difficult.

The paraphernalia of caring for a new baby begins in earnest now. We are surprised to find that everything we bought before he was born is being used. Friends and neighbours visit and we simply don't know what to say to them. Sometimes we tell them the truth and blurt it all out in a clumsy sort of way, and we then find we have to deal with their own feelings of embarrassment. This usually involves making light of the whole thing and reassuring them that things could be much more terrible. Or we don't tell them and wonder if they have noticed that he is different in some way, and this makes us feel even worse sometimes. It is trial and error.

My father-in-law, in his quiet way, is working on our behalf, and has sought out the best specialist in the land for us to see. We go up to London and wait for ages and are ushered into a large room with an oldish man sitting behind a desk surrounded by about twelve people in white coats. They look at us with blank, disinterested faces. We sit down in two chairs opposite all these people. The specialist tells us about mongolism or 'Down's Disease'. It is to do with a chromosome abnormality. James will be slow. But he tells us that mongols tend to have extroverted personalities, and in fact they can be quite rewarding to bring up. He describes the special educational facilities which are available, and in fact seems more optimistic than the other doctor we have seen. He says that at least we know what we have got and we can see the point of that idea, even though it confirms things in a way. We learn that James' condition is quite common and that it is nothing whatever to do with us. This interview lasts about twenty minutes and is really quite helpful. We leave, feeling we know a bit more, but still not totally accepting our situation.

By now I am established at college. One day I am browsing through the library and my eye catches a book on congenital abnormality. I look through the index and see the word 'mongol'. I turn up the page and there find a picture of the hand of a Down's syndrome person. The caption draws attention to the palm creases and the little finger. There is only one line running across the latter. I put the book back on the shelf and go straight home to the flat which we have at last managed to find. We look at James's little finger and see that, indeed, there is just the one line.

This is a final confirmation. James is a mongol.

All parents of handicapped children must experience to some degree the distress and grief about the loss of their normal child that I experienced fourteen years ago and that even now swim into focus as we live our lives together. It seems extraordinary that it is possible to feel so strongly about a tiny baby who is not yet a person, yet the confusion and bewilderment of those first few weeks will remain, remembered as if they were yesterday. That sense of being different from everyone else, of learning to accept the unacceptable, of needing an explanation when none will be complete enough to prove beyond doubt that one is not responsible — these are things that all of us who have gone through the experience have felt in the first few weeks. Fear of the unknown, of the 'monster' we may or may not have created, and feelings of total failure and utter disappointment will compound the ambivalence surrounding parental attitudes to the stark fact of handicap.

What has a handicapped child done to deserve such a range of reactions which are so uncomfortably close to complete rejection? The answer of course, is nothing. Rationally we cannot blame our handicapped children for their incompleteness. Yet the compulsion to seek explanations and to make someone responsible is very strong in many of us. This presents a problem. When there is a diagnosis at birth we cannot focus our anger and frustration on what the child has done, only on what he *is*, or perhaps more accurately on notions of what he may become, gathered from hearsay, gossip, the media and so on. There is thus a huge gap between our knowledge of our child as he is and what he might one day be, which can be filled with a distorted range of attitudes and feelings towards the world, which may have little foundation in reality, but which are nonetheless *real*.

All this has implications for the ways in which professional helpers of one sort or another set about trying to assist in the crisis of the discovery of handicap. There must be a range of professional reactions to us which are complex and hugely varied, but overall it is possible to describe a kind of continuum. At one end there is what appears to be complete cold disinterest; at the other, the communication of a warmth and concern which can assist us in the struggle to come to terms and make something positive of the situation. Midge and I, for example, were quite simply left to get on with it. Whilst I am sure that old attitudes are being displaced, there are still enough horror stories around to show that the kind of callousness which was meted out to us when we first found out about James is still very much a part of the professional care scene. I find it difficult to shake off this expectation, despite the fact that it has been belied many times by professionals who are aware and sensitive. Damage has been done.

Any attempt to try to describe some notion of good helping practice — letting parents feel understood at a level that will help them to grow in their new-found role as parents of handicapped children — must focus on the kind of transactions that take place between the two sides in an equation which is, as it were, equal but different. Parents may have very difficult personal problems to overcome. New dimensions to their personalities may be discovered which may or may not help them to cope with what has happened. Grief and mourning reactions will have to be worked through and possibly sustained over time. Above all the sense of loss and associated feelings of depression will be very strong. All this may or may not affect the professionals involved. But it is clear to me that if our own intimate experience is seen by us not to have any impact on those who seek to help us then we will withdraw and be even more difficult to reach than ever. Yet it is embarrassing for people to stand by while those in distress express their grief openly, and difficult to let them to so without fear of rejection.

Professionals may need to protect themselves from the impact of our distress by seeming hard, callous and insensitive. The parents' distress can, in my view, become equally a part of the equation, experienced and shared helpfully by all involved. In this view, professional helping relationships can be deepened and made hugely more rewarding by the humaneness of what goes on when one person quite simply sits down with another and offers open comfort and understanding.

All this is not to suggest that all that parents need is some form of wishy-washy counselling service, concerned only with our emotional needs. We have rights to practical assistance as well, and the professionals have a duty to spell out what these are. Later, also, there will be an important need for practical, firm, hard-headed straight advice, designed to help us to manage our children's special difficulties. But when talking about the first few days or even hours after the diagnosis has been made, there will be a deep need for professionals to be available, without the hassle of appointments and red tape, simply to stand by, to wait for the inevitable signs of emotional reaction to what has happened and to respond appropriately.

In everything that happens mistakes may be made and risks have to be taken. Yet I am convinced that parents will be able to forgive the professional blunders of the doctors, nurses, social workers and health visitors when they occur if they approach us with respect, consideration, warmth and care. If these qualities are missing then we may seek revenge, emerging in the form of parental hostility and disrespect which may not be expressed openly but can turn inward, confirming us in our guilt, reinforcing our failure and deepening those feelings of depression and misery that are so debilitating and destructive of human potential.

# Glossary of Medical Terms

|  |  |
|---|---|
| Amniocentesis | drawing off a sample of the fluid that surrounds a baby in its mother's womb |
| Anti-depressants | drugs used to treat depression |
| Caesarian section | delivering a baby by surgical opening of the womb |
| Carcinoma | cancer |
| Chromosome | that element in the body cell which determines its behaviour and structure |
| Colostomy | an operation to create an opening from the large bowel to the abdominal surface |
| Down's syndrome | a group of congenital abnormalities with definite characteristics known as Mongolism |
| Electro-encephalogram | a recording of the intrinsic electrical activity of the brain |
| Genetic counselling | giving information about the risks of inherited disease |
| Haemorrhage | bleeding |
| Heart failure | failure of the heart to function normally |
| Hirschsprung's disease | a condition in babies in which a segment of the lower bowel does not dilate to allow the passage of the stools, thereby causing an obstruction |
| Laparotomy | an operation opening the abdominal cavity |
| Apnoea | failure to breathe |
| Pulmonary hypertension | high blood pressure in the circulation through the lungs |
| Radio-therapy | treatment using irradiation |
| Respiratory help | help with breathing |

125

| | |
|---|---|
| Spina bifida | a defect at the base of the spine often involving the spinal nerve causing paralysis and bladder problems |
| Sterilization | a surgical operation to prevent conception permanently |
| Still born | born dead |
| Ventricular Septal Defect | a hole between the two main chambers of the heart |
| Ventilate | cause to breathe by mechanical means |
| Viral meningitis | inflammation of the lining of the brain due to a virus |

# Index

Allen family, 9–12, 15–16, 58, 62–4
Anderson, Neil, 91, 93, 95, 97, 103
Anderson, Philip, 91, 97
Anderson family, 77, 80–81, 91–3, 95, 97, 101–102
Anthony, Sylvia, 109
Arnold, Matthew, 8

Ballard, Midge, 115–20, 123
Ballard, Rod, vii, 115–24
Binger, C. M., 94
Birth of handicapped child, vii, 1–2, 5–6, 9–11, 12–13, 16, 19, 37, 40, 43–4, 62–4, 118–22; see also Grief
Bonding: parent-child, 2, 22, 36–7, 57–8; professional, 60
Bowlby, John, 110
British Medical Journal, 3
Brompton Hospital, 49
Brown, Dr, 9, 11, 40–3, 72
Burton, Lindy, 91–2

Cann family, 37–9, 68, 72–3
Caplan, Gerald, 82–3
Cooper, Mrs, 8, 61
Coping, with family crisis, 31–4, 48, 57, 71, 76, 82–90, 103;

denial of illness, 79–80, 83, 84–5; family functioning, 83, 86–8, 99–100, 104–5, 108–9, 111–12; response of ill child, 88, 94–101; response of parents, 82–6, 88, 103–7, 113, 118–24; response of siblings, 87, 90–93, 98, 103–5, 109–10; see also Families; Grief
Cot death, 54–5
Cystic fibrosis, 87, 92

Dante Alighieri, 36
D'Arcy, E., 3
Death: child's awareness of, 93, 108–9; family response after, 111–12; of handicapped child, vii, 8, neonatal, 6, 8, 11–13, 16–18, 20–4, 27, 57–8, 61, 65, older child, 30, 34, 50–6, 59, 71–2; parents' response to, 103–7; siblings' response to, 93, 109–10
Depression, 21, 28–9, 42, 62, 97, 123–4
Dickens, Charles, viii
Down's syndrome, 37–8, 40, 43–51, 54, 68, 70, 73, 118–24
Drew, Damien, 85, 96, 109
Drew, Gerald, 85

Drew, Richard, 85
Drew family, 77, 85, 89, 96
Drugs, side-effects of, 78–9, 88, 105, 109, 113

Elfer, Peter, vii, 75–113

Family functioning, 83, 86–8, 99–100, 104–5, 108–9, 111–112
Families: at birth, 2–6, 9–11, 12, 15–17, 19, 25–7, 37–9, 62–5, 71–3, 113; in crisis, 31–4, 48, 57, 71, 75–6; at death, 6–8, 11–12, 17–18, 20, 23–4, 27, 30, 34, 52–4; involvement of parents, 88, 99, 104, 113; later support given, 11–12, 14–16, 24–5, 27–30, 34–6, 38–44, 47–8, 55–61, 69, 82–8, 108–9, 123–4; need for social work support, vii–viii, 2, 6–8, 58–9; openness about terminal illness, 76, 87–8, 92–3, 104–5; support services, 21, 42, 51, 68; treatment of and diagnosis given, 2–12, 16, 22–3, 36–40, 44–6, 48, 51, 55–65, 70–3, 76, 79–83, 118–19; *see also* Coping with family crisis; Grief
Family network, *see* Relatives
Fathers, needs of, 10–12, 33, 44–6, 49, 58, 62, 71–2
Fergus, Dr, 31, 33–4, 37–8, 44, 48–9, 72–3
Field family, 16–18, 66
Friedman, S. B., 85

Genetic counselling, 11, 18, 25

Green, M., 103
Green family, 18–21, 58, 66
Grief, 25–30, 31–3, 57, 60, 65, 67; at death, 6–7, 11–12, 14, 16, 18, 21–2, 35, 48, 50, 54–6, 58–9, 104, 106–7, 111–12; for lost healthy child, vii, 4–8, 9–12, 16, 21, 38–9, 42, 46, 50, 84, 89–90, 122–3
Guilt, feelings of, 18–19, 21, 51–2, 59, 65, 84, 89–91, 107, 124

Handicapped child: birth of, vii, 1–2, 5–6, 9–13, 16, 19, 37, 40, 43–4, 62–4; death of, vii, 6, 8, 11–13, 16–18, 20–4, 27, 50–9, 61, 65, 68–72; initial diagnosis, 1–6, 36–9, 40–1, 44–6, 48, 118–122; rearing of, 60, 72–3; support services, 42, 51
Harris family, 25–30, 57, 67–8
Heart defects, 16, 25–7, 48–9, 52, 54–5, 68
Hollis, 76
Hospitalization, child's response to, 95–6, 100–102

Jacobs, Edward, 92
Jacobs, Ian, 92
Jacobs, Tina, 94, 99
Jacobs family, 77, 88–9, 92
Jones, Dr, 16–20, 22–5, 27–8, 51, 54

Kennell, J., 36
Kew, S., 3
Kingston, John, 105, 110
Kingston, Mary, 105, 109–10

Kingston family, 77, 84–5, 87, 89, 104–6, 111
Klaus, M., 36

Leukaemia, vii, 75–113; child's problems, 88, 94–103, 108–9; family problems, 75–7, 84, 90–3, 98–101; lymphoblastic leukaemia, 75, 78–9; myeloblastic leukaemia, 78; remission of, 79, 84–5, 103; telling the child, 76, 93, 95–6, 98, 108; treatment of, 78–9, 81, 84–8, 95–9, 101, 103–4, 106, 113; *see also* Coping with family crisis; Drugs, side-effects of; Families; Radiotherapy
Long, Patricia, 80, 92
Long, Terence, 92
Long family, 77, 80–1, 83, 92
Lonsdale, Gill, vii

McAndrew, I., 3
Marital stress, 8, 12, 15, 47, 49, 61–2
Martin, Dr, 48, 51–3
Masters, Mrs, 77, 82, 96, 101, 104, 106
Mathews, Mrs, 77, 89, 92
Maturity, increased (leukaemia children), 101–2
Memories of dead child, 6, 11, 15, 18, 26–7, 30, 35, 53; *see also* Grief
Meningitis, viral, 30
Mongol, mongolism, *see* Down's syndrome
Morrisey, J., 101
Mourning, *see* Grief

Old family, 8, 61–2
Olshansky, Simon, 108

Parker family, 44–50, 68, 70–71
Philips, Sarah, 95
Philips family, 77, 81, 84, 95, 113
Pinkus, Lily, 107

Radiotherapy, 78–9, 97
Ramsey, Michael, 56
Rankin, Dr, 119
Regression (leukaemia children), 101–2, 105
Relatives, involvement of, 8, 10, 17, 30–5, 58–9, 62, 64, 68
Roberts family, 50–6, 68–70
Robinson, Margaret, 82
Rodgers, James, 80, 90
Rodgers family, 77, 80, 88, 90, 92, 104, 106–7
Rosenblatt, B., 110
Ross, Alan O., 79, 86, 90

Saunders, Cecily, 108
Separation: of baby and mother, 5, 36–7, 39, 68; of ill child from family, 96, 109
Social workers: in crisis, 31–4, 48–50, 57, 68, 71, 103–4, 106, 112–13; at death, 6–7, 11, 13–14, 16, 20–21, 24, 27, 34, 51–3, 57; evaluation of, 63–4, 67, 69–73, 81; later support of parents, 11, 14–16, 24–5, 27–30, 34–6, 38–43, 47–8, 51, 54–61, 67, 69, 71–3, 83–6, 91–3, 123–4; role of, vii–viii, 1–2, 6–8, 58–9, 100; support of leukaemia child, 94–6, 98–101,

108–9; telling parents of initial diagnosis, 2–5, 7–11, 15–17, 19–20, 22–4, 25–6, 37–40, 44–6, 51, 57–8, 63, 66–7, 70, 80–2

Spina bifida baby, 8–15, 62, 65

Stephens family, 40–4, 68, 71–2

Stokes, B. M., 36

Team approach to illness and handicap, 3–7, 15–16, 24, 30, 37, 39–40, 57, 59–60, 67, 71, 80, 88, 98; parents' part in, 88

Temple, Brian, 105, 110

Temple, Michael, 92, 105, 109–10

Temple, Steven, 92, 100, 105, 109

Temple family, 77, 84, 90, 92, 100, 106, 111

Thomas, Christine, 100

Thomas, Linda, 88, 100

Thomas family, 77, 80–1, 85, 87–90, 100

Thompson family, 22–5, 66–7

Thorpe, Richard, 30–6, 68

Thorpe family, 30–6, 68

Tolstoy, Leo, 1

Turk, J., 87

Whiten, A., 36

Wickens, Mathew, 84, 90, 108

Wickens family, 77, 83–5, 90, 105–6, 111

Wilkes, Eileen, 43

Wilkes, John, 43

Williams family, 12–16, 64–6

Wolff, Sula, 101–2